The Most Incredible Real Estate Money Making Gift on the Planet Guaranteed ($1,966.94 Value)!

FREE

Jam-Packed with everything you see here. Limited Time Offer. Act Now!

($1,966.94 Value)

Incredible Free Gift Part 1 of 3

12 Free Months of Brian's "Ultimate Make Money Hotsheet" mailed to your doorstep, no strings attached. ($297 value)!

Incredible Free Gift Part 2 of 3

Free CD Download: 1 Hr. Interview with Brian about his 5 Guaranteed Steps to Small Business Success ($49 value)!
"This is the most powerful interview I've ever done." - Brian Evans

Incredible Free Gift Part 3 of 3

Free 30 minute 1-on-1 Make Money in Real Estate Jump Start Conference Call withBrian Evans. (value = Priceless)!
Students have said that this call was the most important and influential call of their entire real estate investing career. Brian typically charges $500/hr for consultations, however for a limited time you can speak to him FREE.

Course Manual and CD Set, "The 77 Biggest Mistakes Real Estate Investors Make ($997 value)!
The quality of information contained in this course is so content rich that everyone from those just starting, all the way up to the established real estate investor will benefit from the proven methods and mistakes to avoid.

Brian's Library of his 50 Most Commonly Used Real Estate Investing Forms ($387 value)!
This is a CD-Rom which you can put in your computer and print forms out at your leisure. Be sure to have your attorney review and approve the forms and make them "your state friendly."

Lifetime Access to "Foreclosure Gold Rush Live" Website ($39.97 value)!
If you've ever entertained the thought of investing in real estate and making a tremendous fortune in foreclosures, then this online program will show you the secrets.

Everything You Need To Attract Private Lenders ($147 value)!
I give you the most common and essential documents that I use to attract and work with private mortgage lenders in my real estate investing business. When utilized properly, private lenders will make you a lot of money and in return you'll provide them a very good return on investment.

Six Month Access to "What Would Evans Do" (WWED) Fax Back Hotline (value = Priceless)!
Have questions that need answers? No problem. Send your questions to my fax back hotline and I'l respond to you usually within 24 hours. This gift allows you to get inside my head, and therefore I can't even begin to put a price tag on this.

more

One Full Month Membership to Ultimate Real Estate Investors VIP Membership ($49.97 value)!

THIS IS THE ULTIMATE PLACE where Real Estate Investors from all over North America come together to Make Money, Live Wealthy, No Excuses."

TOP SECRET MONTHLY "VIP NEWSLETTERS" 20+ page Newsletters, referred to as a day long intense seminar in print arriving by first class mail.

EXCLUSIVE CD's OF THE MONTH. These are exclusive monthly CD's about keeping up with what's new, and other how to make money in real estate (without money, credit, or experience) tips.

SPECIAL VIP OPEN LINE WEEKLY CONFERENCE CALLS. Get first hand advice with weekly call in times to discuss deals, asset protection, contracts, sellers, buyers, etc!

NEW → *PARTNERSHIP PROFITS. If you want, I will personally partner with you on your real estate deals: helping you get commitments, structure contracts, and close your deals. My personal money may or may not be used, case by case.*

DEAL STRUCTURING ADVICE. Each month you can fill out my UPS (Ultimate Prescreening Sellers) Sheet or my UPB (Ultimate Prescreening Buyers) Sheet and fax them to my office for direct input on how you should approach and structure each deal that you are considering. It's like having a real estate angel on your shoulder!

VIP MEMBERS' RESTRICTED ACCESS WEBSITE: A section of the website contains past issues of the TOP SECRET VIP Newsletter, articles, special news, etc. ONLY VIP Members are given the access code for this website.

CONTINUALLY UP-DATED "MILLION DOLLAR RESOURCE DIRECTORY: There are contacts and resources that myself and clients use - and in many cases, have found only after diligent and difficult search.

20% DISCOUNT ON FUTURE PRODUCTS AND EVENTS

OTHER SPECIAL PERKS and call in hours ONLY for VIP Members

************** **I TOLD YOU IT WAS INCREDIBLE!** **************

There is a one-time charge of $19.95 to cover shipping and handling for everything with free gift 3 of 3. After your 1 month free test drive as a VIP Member you will automatically continue at the lowest VIP Member price of $49.97 per month. Should you decide to cancel your membership, you can do so at any time by calling our office at 859-309-1714. Remember, your credit card will NOT be charged the low monthly membership fee until the begining of the 2nd month, which means you will receive 1 full month of all benefits outlined above to read, test, and profit from all of the powerful techniques and strategies you get from being an Ultimate Real Estate Investor "VIP" Member. **You Can't Lose Guarantee** - And of course, it's impossible for you to lose, because if you don't absolutely LOVE everything you get, simply call 859-309-1714 and we'll even refund your S&H.

*EMAIL REQUIRED IN ORDER TO NOTIFY YOU ABOUT YOUR ORDER

Full Name

Billing Address

City   State   Zip   *Email

Phone   Fax

Credit Card Instructions to Cover $19.95 Shipping & Handling:

_____Visa   _____MasterCard   _____American Express   _____Discover

Credit Card Number:_____ Exp. Date_____

Signature_____ Date_____

Providing this information constitutes your permission for Ultimate Real Estate Investors to contact you regarding related information via mail, email, fax and phone. Your Credit Card Statement should reflect a charge from BrianEvansSupport.com

Order Online at www.FreeMakeMoneyGift.com
Or Fax Back to 859-201-1441
Or Mail To: 3070 Lakecrest Circle 400-260 Lexington, KY 40513

HOW TO
MAKE MONEY
IN YOUR LOCAL
REAL ESTATE
MARKET

HOW TO
MAKE MONEY
IN YOUR LOCAL
REAL ESTATE
MARKET

Start Investing Without Money,

Credit or Experience

BRIAN T. EVANS, JR.

Published by Advantage, Charleston, South Carolina.
Member of Advantage Media Group.

ADVANTAGE is a registered trademark and the Advantage colophon is a trademark of Advantage Media Group, Inc.

Printed in the United States of America.

ISBN: 978-1-59932-205-6
LCCN: 2010909674

This publication is designed to provide accurate and authoritative information in regard to the subject matter covered. It is sold with the understanding that the publisher is not engaged in rendering legal, accounting, or other professional services. If legal advice or other expert assistance is required, the services of a competent professional person should be sought.

Most Advantage Media Group titles are available at special quantity discounts for bulk purchases for sales promotions, premiums, fundraising, and educational use. Special versions or book excerpts can also be created to fit specific needs.

For more information, please write: Special Markets, Advantage Media Group, P.O. Box 272, Charleston, SC 29402 or call 1.866.775.1696.

Visit us online at **advantagefamily**.com

Dedication

It would be unfair for me to attempt an expression of gratitude to each loving and influential individual in my life with just a few simple words on a page. Therefore, to my family, friends, and mentors, please consider this an all-encompassing "thank you" for your love, friendship, guidance and support. It is worth more to me than anything in this world.

To my wife, Danielle, the one person in my life who took a vow to stand by me day in, day out, for richer or poorer, through sickness and health, till death do us part, I thank you. You will be my best friend and the love of my life to the end of time.

And lastly, to you the reader, may my words inspire you to turn your real estate investing dreams into reality and make the impossible possible.

Table of Contents

The Big Picture to Real Estate Investing

The Five Steps to Ultimate Success When Buying Houses

The Five Steps to Ultimate Success When Selling Houses

The Big Picture Mind Map

Marketing Your Business

Additional Methods to Find Deals

Understand Your Market

Always Focus on Revenue

Three Primary Habits You Need to Implement

Why Investors Get a Bad Rap

Do What You Say

Don't Be Afraid to Annoy People

Be a Fighter Pilot

Questionnaire

The Professional Support Team of an Ultimate Real Estate Investor

Team Member 1: Real Estate Agent

Team Member 2: Mortgage Broker

Team Member 3: Real Estate Business Attorney

Team Member 4: Title Company/Closing Attorney

Disclosure

You understand and agree that there are important risk factors that should be considered when deciding to invest in real estate.

NO EARNINGS PROJECTIONS, PROMISES, OR REPRESENTATIONS

You recognize and agree that we have made no implications, warranties, promises, suggestions, projections, representations, or guarantees whatsoever to you about future prospects or earnings or that you will earn any money, with respect to your purchase of this book, and that we have not authorized any such projection, promise, or representation by others.

YOUR SUCCESS – OR LACK THEREOF

Your success in using the information or strategies provided in this book depends on a variety of factors. We have no way of knowing how well you will do, as we do not know you, your background, your work ethic, your dedication, your motivation, your desire, or your business skills or practices. Therefore, we do not guarantee or imply that you will get rich, that you will do as well, or that you will receive any earnings at all.

Real estate-related businesses and earnings involve unknown risks and are not suitable for everyone. You may not rely on any information presented in this book, or otherwise provided by us, unless you do so with the knowledge and understanding that you can experience significant losses including, but not limited to, the loss of any monies spent starting, operating, and/or marketing your real estate investment business.

DUE DILIGENCE

You are advised to do your own due diligence when it comes to making business decisions and should use caution and seek the advice of qualified professionals. You should check with your accountant, lawyer, and professional financial advisor before acting on this or any information. You may not consider any examples, documents, or other content in this book, on Web sites herein, or otherwise provided by us to be the equivalent of legal, tax, or financial advice. We assume no responsibility for any losses or damages resulting from your use of any information, or opportunity contained within this book's materials and Web site or within any information disclosed by the owner of the book in any form whatsoever.

Preface

Do you ever feel like you are working too hard for your living ... not getting ahead fast enough? Perhaps everything you are doing as an aspiring or established entrepreneur feels like one step forward and two steps back. My name is Brian Evans and I would like to introduce myself and my book by answering the following three questions: (1) Who is this book for? (2) What is this book about? (3) Why should you read this book?

WHO IS THIS BOOK FOR?

This book is for…

- The small-business owner who is "working too hard to make a living" or always worrying about where the next customers are coming from.

- Owners, presidents, executives of midsize companies frustrated with slow growth, tough and "cheap-price" competition, wondering where your next big business breakthrough might come from.

- Men and women stuck in unfulfilling jobs, eager to own their own businesses, to find new opportunities, to go from "9 to 5" to "MY OWN BOSS", to do something interesting and exciting.

- Sales professionals struggling to gain ground ... weary of "cold" prospecting, tired of fighting just to get an opportunity to sell, thinking, "there must be a better way."

- E-commerce and Internet savvy people with the ambition to use their knowledge for profit.

- Even authors, speakers, coaches and consultants will be blown away by the opportunities, strategies, by the whole world they didn't know existed, its doors thrown open wide, with real estate.

- And ANYONE who simply wants to get more done, to make more money, grow massive wealth, to act with greater confidence, to think more creatively, even to be healthier, more in control of their life and future.

WHAT IS THIS BOOK ABOUT?

Before I tell you what this book is about, allow me to first tell you what it is NOT about. It is not about a business similar to rocket science, or a business that requires a sixth sense. Nor does it require money, credit, or previous experience to achieve millionaire success.

Simply put, this book is about…

- How to buy, sell, and grow massive wealth in real estate with no money, credit, or experience.

- Becoming your local real estate investing expert and creating multiple income streams through investing techniques such as "subject-to," "short sale," "seller financing," "wholesaling," "lease option," "option," "self-directed IRA," "private lenders," "land trusts," "retailing," "land contract," and this list goes on. (Don't worry if those terms don't make sense yet, they will!)

- Making money in real estate based on the knowledge and creativity you have, not based on the checks you write, or the checks you think you have to write.

- Starting and systemizing a real estate investing business that allows you to cash big checks no matter what the economy is doing.

- Learning a new skill that will greatly benefit your life, your children's lives, and your grandchildren's lives.

- How to get to the first level or the next level as a real estate investor.

- How to gain control of the finances in your life and turn the cash flow faucet up or down based on your personal needs or desires.

WHY SHOULD YOU READ THIS BOOK?

It doesn't matter if you are black, white, red, or yellow. It doesn't matter if you have $100 in your bank account or $1,000,000. We all put our pants on one leg at a time, we all enjoy a good dinner and a movie, we all go to bed at night and wake up to the same sun the next day. We are all 99.99% physically the same.

What makes all readers of this book different and keeps you going personally in business and life, during times when 99.99% of others would give up, is an inner drive to be the best at what you do, to be a good person, and work hard to grow the business and the lifestyle of your dreams.

You may be wondering why you should consider taking the time to be a real estate investor when you already have so many other things going on in your life. It's a fair question, and I have a fair answer for you: because you deserve to finally reap the financial rewards of your daily efforts, and this won't happen if you are stuck in a dead-end job, working 9-to-5, living month to month off your current paycheck.

No matter how much you wish for change, things will always stay the same unless you take action and make an effort to try something new and exciting, like real estate investing.

As for me, personally, I wasn't born with a silver spoon in my mouth. I had to bust my butt, out-think my competitors, invest in my education, and work hard every single day to get what I have, and I still do. Was it easy to get to where I am today? Of course not; in fact, to be honest with you, it was probably the hardest thing I've ever had to endure, but worth every second.

This book is for you if you want the author to provide you with ...

- Honesty and integrity
- Clear explanations
- Sometimes harsh reality
- Proven systems for income and wealth
- Simple yet effective tasks, and to-do's
- Real life examples
- Insider information
- Tools and resources you can use today
- Advice on what not to do
- Greater control and independence
- Revitalized confidence

If you're ready for NEW opportunity, you've definitely found yourself in the right place at the right time. If you're ready for that supercharged and creative experience that'll get your real estate entre-preneurial juices flowing like never before, then you're going to be THRILLED that you purchased this book!

If you're frustrated with being a victim of the real estate investing industry's smoke and mirror secrets about what it really takes to become successful in this business that other trainers don't share with you, then Do NOT blame yourself, because it isn't your fault. I promise to show you that you can learn the secrets to the real estate magicians' tricks, which will allow you to BECOME AN ULTIMATE REAL ESTATE INVESTOR.

You should be motivated like never before in your life by the epic real estate investing opportunities lying right in front of you every single day. If you are already an established real estate investor then perhaps this book will entice you to reinvent your real estate investing business 100% for the better. Ultimately, my motive is simply this … I want to help you. It really is this simple. I am passionate about getting this message out all across the country, and I hope you will somehow sense my sincerity and love for real estate investing within this book and be motivated by the information to take your dreams to the next level. I know from personal experience that you will see the light about the business of real estate, and be richer, safer, smarter, and happier as a result of this new knowledge that I'm offering you here.

You'll learn how to turn an ordinary business into an extraordinary business. How to immunize and insulate yourself in a down market. How to dramatically increase your income, how to instantly decrease your stress, and how to make your real estate business your servant rather than your master.

If you would love to gain millionaire status as a real estate investor then you are about to tap into your inner genius to become smarter, more progressive, more aggressive and develop a true love for real estate investing, along with a new and sincere desire to get rich and richer (with no apologies for doing so). I will help you develop an optimistic, forward-looking attitude and share with you timely information (based on my real-life experiences) about what's working today.

If you would value discovering and connecting with a teacher, trainer, coach, author, and advisor who wasn't invented yesterday on the Internet ... who has actually built a solid real estate investing business from scratch ...who has a track record ... who routinely cashes large checks from real estate deals over and over and can prove it ... then you and I are about to become fast friends.

I happen to admire, respect, and, yes, care for the great real estate entrepreneur! In this day and age, when government drama and media talking heads are openly attacking and demonizing this business, it seems to me somebody needs to stand as a voice for and be an encourager and supporter of the real heroes of our economy, which are YOU, the entrepreneurs.

I am so unbelievably certain of the value of the content that I am providing to you here today and so convinced that real estate investors all over the country NEED to know these secrets before it is too late. Ultimately, my friend, it's virtually impossible for you to learn what I can teach you for even a fraction of the cost.

If you put my proven strategies into play in your business and do not see a direct increase in money earned and money saved over a full 12-month period, then write me a letter and I'll gladly send you a refund for the cost of this book.

I want you to know that as a committed and self-made millionaire entrepreneur I have written this book for you in an effort to share my experiences and help you succeed as a real estate investor. In fact, I would wager that you and I are not all that different. Real estate investing is my favorite vehicle for building wealth, and since you are reading this book, I bet it is yours too. It is definitely a passion of mine, and unless you are prepared to talk real estate with me, I would oftentimes prefer not talk at all. I've bought and sold hundreds of properties using a variety of proven and creative investment strategies. Much of my base knowledge has come from training and learning from a variety of sources over many years. Therefore, I am a huge proponent of ongoing personal education. I've read and continue to read numerous books on real estate and other business ventures. I can honestly say that I've started at the bottom and worked my way up, and firmly believe that you are never too young or old to learn new things.

From my own evaluated experiences, I have decided to take the skills and systems that I've established and share this information with others. I believe one of the major keys to my continued success as a real estate investor is my commitment to facing my fears and pushing the limits of my business, and I would like to extend these same principles to you.

What I've found, time and time again, is that the doors for success are always there and always waiting to be opened. I hope you are as excited as I am for you to open these doors and walk through them as you achieve your goals. I know you will enjoy all my real-life stories, secrets, examples and key points within each chapter. I'm here for you throughout your real estate investing journey.

To your ultimate real estate investing success,

Brian T. Evans Jr.

P.S. Here are a just a few testimonials given to me from students who actually implemented the money-making information I provided to them. This is undeniable proof that my simple investing strategies change lives. Will you be next?

Brian,

I smile when I think back over the last few months – first because I finally kicked it into gear, and secondly because you have given me a tremendous gift. You have given me the knowledge that you possess to go out and create some big checks! You are by far the most knowledgeable person when it comes to short sales … hands down! Your talent in other deal structuring and making the business happen is tremendous. Anyone would be so lucky to have you work with them. Look what you have been able to mold me into!

You have instilled in me confidence that I knew "You always had my back" if I got into a situation that I was not sure how to handle, which is so important being new and taking those first steps that can be quite uncomfortable until you've done it a few times.

Thank you for being patient when it was needed, as well as persistent and firm when working with me. I look forward to moving much more swiftly in the next year to reach my ultimate goals for '09 and '10.

All my best,

Elizabeth Lisk

Brian,

I wanted to take a minute and tell you how much I appreciate you! It really is amazing how much has changed since you started mentoring me.

At the time you started helping me with investing I was really stuck, had done three deals over the course of two years, and could not figure out how to put all the pieces together. I was overwhelmed with three young children, no money to invest in marketing and could not get anything consistent going. I was discouraged, confused and did not really know where to start, along with having faced a few deals that had not gone through because I did not have anyone reliable to help me work through them. Real estate investing has a lot of moving parts, and they all need to be going at the same time to have an actual business, as opposed to a hit and miss deal or two.

Since you have been personally working with me, along with the weekly VIP calls, so much has changed. You gave me the idea to get an apprentice – which I did. As a direct result of having an apprentice, I have signs out around town and have a contract on a house with seller financing (zero interest) which will make *me anywhere from $5k to $25k profit. This contract came from a call off a sign and I am currently getting about 6-10 calls a day for buyers, and have received other seller calls as well. I closed a deal a few weeks ago and made $5,000 which was great and really encouraging. That deal came as a result of an investor response from one of my ads. My apprentice is also getting my pre-foreclosure leads pulled weekly and mailing out the marketing for me. He does my marketing at his expense and I answer investing questions for him along with showing him how to close a deal. I am also working multiple short sale leads and actually had to pace myself to make sure I can handle the number of leads that come in.*

It has only been a couple of months, but the difference in my confidence level, having other people do some of the work for me and seeing results are amazing. I actually have a business that is growing, bringing in regular leads that can be built up quickly. I really cannot thank you enough, along with your awesome staff, for all the help you have given and continue to give. I am excited about investing again, my confidence and abilities are growing because I know you have my back and will give me advice that I can trust. There are a lot of people out there who give real estate investing advice, but to have someone who is so trustworthy is rare. I am really looking forward to all the deals that are in the works, including one currently which should bring a profit of about $70,000 because of your advice. Thank you for the opportunity to be mentored by you and your consistent and gracious support.

With much gratitude,

Jo Amick

Hi Brian,

I received a package the other day and the VIP Newsletter for Ultimate Real Estate Investors. I read the section on private money 10 must-know tips to easily getting private money. And what I did NOT get was any hype, fluff or BS. Now that within itself is saying something worthwhile, and newsworthy!

I am going to make time to read through this and safe keep it for future reading. This information is more than I can begin to talk about here! I'll read it and share what I learned after I put some of the tips into action. By the way your office manager Mrs. Calisa Fitzpatrick is very professional and considerate, and she is one of the best follow-up callers in the country, and I sincerely mean that.

I have been in the real estate arena for seven years or more and I have just about all of the programs out there and to be honest I am not feeling it like I am with your information, and your staff support, that means a lot, as you know! Whatever you have available, it is good, and I want to be associated with your VIP network of investors. There are a few that I can recall that I have their material but they can not be reached at times, maybe through email support which is fine, but nothing can beat a phone conversation if time permits, so thank you!

All the best to you and those close to you,

Don

Foreword

By Ron LeGrand

There are few people whom I might actually endorse these days, let alone take the time to write a foreword for their book, but Brian Evans is one of them. I first met Brian in 2007 at one of my seminars. He was already a "mover and shaker" real estate investor, but, like all super-successful investors, his ever-increasing thirst for new knowledge brought us together and kept us friends.

Brian was a flat-broke southern boy from Kentucky, turned Wall Street dropout, turned failed retail coffee shop owner, turned real estate investor, turned millionaire real estate expert, author, speaker, and mentor by the age of 28. Oh yeah, and he still invests in real estate full time, doing anywhere from two to six houses per month, with more than 25 deals working at any given time, and a resume of deals totaling in the hundreds.

He is now married with kids on the way, lives in a gorgeous 25-acre, million-dollar estate in Lexington that backs up to the Kentucky River. Clearly, he is someone you need to listen to when it comes to real estate investing and entrepreneurial success.

As you read this book, you will discover real-life insider secrets to making serious money as a real estate investor, growing wealth, establishing a real business rather than a come-and-go infomercial business, and, ultimately, becoming a millionaire real estate investor. Brian has laid out the information in such a way that anyone who can read this book can gain a tremendous grasp of what it really takes to make it big.

So grab a pen, a highlighter, and a comfortable seat as you enjoy devouring every inspiring moneymaking word in Brian's powerful book.

Sincerely,

Ron LeGrand

Author, *How to Be a Quick Turn Real Estate Millionaire*
Author, *Fast Cash with Quick Turn Real Estate*

CHAPTER 1

The Big Picture to Real Estate Investing

While I'm not here to offer you the next and greatest technique on how to profit from a booming foreclosure market or get into the fine mathematics of real estate finance or the intricacies of land development, I am going to discuss what I believe is the foundation for success and longevity as a real estate investor.

First, some good news. Real estate investing isn't rocket science but *simple math* and a *simple system*. I don't care whether you are a seasoned investor or a rookie investor, you can make serious money in this business if you, first and foremost, have the right knowledge and mindset. Second, you need to have what I like to call "the flame." This is something the majority of people in this world think they have or wished they had but, unfortunately, they don't. "The flame" is a burning desire deep inside that fuels your ability to take action. I think a lot of people are born with it (lucky for some), but I also think that it is a trait that can be recognized and honed with time. With these two things you can accomplish anything your real estate dreams can conceive and I and many of my students and peers are living proof. Good news for you is that you *can* do it, too!

So who am I and why am I qualified to help you succeed? I thought you would never ask. The fact is I am just a Kentucky southern boy. I was once a broke, paycheck-to-paycheck, no credit, one pair of shoes, take the bus to work every day, 9-to-5 rat-racer who happened to get the desire one day to quit my job and start my own retail coffee shop business with some other "at the time" friends because we thought we could dethrone Starbucks with our premium Kona-style blend.

Boy, I was blindly floating on a cloud. After a few short years and many personally guaranteed debts later, I realized that it was time to jump ship and either get back to the rat race or focus my "flame" on a different goal. You guessed it – I chose real estate investing just as you have.

I read some books on real estate investing and began educating myself about the opportunities available in this business, and I was blown away by the potential that I kept hearing the "gurus" talk about. Then, with a little networking, I found a low-key investor in my area and talked myself into a nonpaying apprenticeship for this investor guy. This turned out to be the boost that I needed to get me started, because I was able to see firsthand by working with this guy that this business wasn't rocket science. But in actuality it is *simple math*.

I quickly realized – and you should, too – that as long as you can sell a property for more than what you are able to buy it for then you will make a *profit*. That's it. In your early days, it doesn't matter if you make $5,000, $10,000, or $40,000 like I did on my first deal. As long as you sell for more that what you buy for, then you make money. And that is why you and I are both in this business: to make money.

But Brian, you're asking, I don't have any money to buy houses with, and don't I need money and credit?

No, Debbie Downer, stop listening to the naysayers and talking heads on TV. You don't have to have money or credit to buy, sell, flip, or lease houses. And even though I told you that you don't need money or credit, some readers may try to find every little reason or excuse in the world to negate what I just said. If this is you, then my best advice is to turn off the news, stop thinking conventionally, and start thinking creatively. Stick with me, and I'll help you see the light – I promise!

My friend, I'm not much of a "real estate psychiatrist" or apologizing for your poor investments, uninspired gurus, or "educational" seminars you lost money on. The fact is, I've been there, too, and if a broke country boy from Kentucky can find his way to the top, so can you. I can look you in the eye and tell you the truth that this business *is* tough, that it is *not* a get-rich-quick business but a get-rich-quicker-than-other-businesses business. If you read and study and implement the real-life information that I provide in this book, then you will succeed and make a lot of money. But if you don't, then you might as well pack your real estate investing bags now, because it probably isn't going to happen for you. Sorry for harsh reality, but you'll thank me later.

Now, get your highlighter ready because I am about to share with you "the secret," the blueprint to buying houses, the key to selling houses, the treasure map to your first deal, or your first million-dollar year.

There are five steps to success as a real estate investor, and if you stray from any of these five steps, you will not succeed. However, if you follow these five steps that I share with you, regardless of what type of deal you pursue, you will succeed. It's only a matter of time.

THE FIVE STEPS TO ULTIMATE SUCCESS WHEN BUYING HOUSES

Step 1: Locate Prospects

Step 2: Prescreen Prospects

Step 3: Construct and Present Offers

Step 4: Follow Up and Get a Commitment

Step 5: Close Quickly and Repeat

THE FIVE STEPS TO ULTIMATE SUCCESS WHEN SELLING HOUSES

Step 1: Locate Prospects

Step 2: Prescreen Prospects

Step 3: Construct and Present Offers

Step 4: Follow Up and Get a Commitment

Step 5: Close Quickly and Repeat

Notice any similarities between the steps to follow when buying houses and selling houses? The Big Picture process is exactly the same on the front end as on the back end. Don't complicate this business or try to invalidate what I am explaining, because this is important for you to understand.

THE BIG PICTURE MIND MAP

If the Big Picture (five steps) still isn't transparent enough, this mind map will give you a visual explanation:

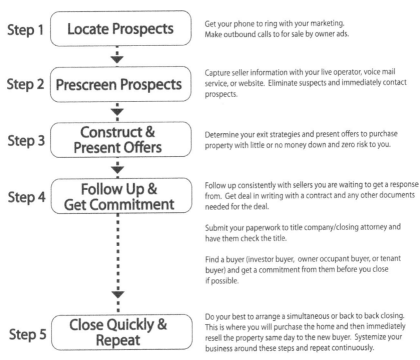

The BIG Picture
(Mind Map)

Step 1 — Locate Prospects
Get your phone to ring with your marketing. Make outbound calls to for sale by owner ads.

Step 2 — Prescreen Prospects
Capture seller information with your live operator, voice mail service, or website. Eliminate suspects and immediately contact prospects.

Step 3 — Construct & Present Offers
Determine your exit strategies and present offers to purchase property with little or no money down and zero risk to you.

Step 4 — Follow Up & Get Commitment
Follow up consistently with sellers you are waiting to get a response from. Get deal in writing with a contract and any other documents needed for the deal.

Submit your paperwork to title company/closing attorney and have them check the title.

Find a buyer (investor buyer, owner occupant buyer, or tenant buyer) and get a commitment from them before you close if possible.

Step 5 — Close Quickly & Repeat
Do your best to arrange a simultaneous or back to back closing. This is where you will purchase the home and then immediately resell the property same day to the new buyer. Systemize your business around these steps and repeat continuously.

In my office, we follow these same five steps *every day* when buying and selling properties, and we have more than 25 deals happening at any given time. Yes, there are some nuances to each of these five steps, but what I'm giving you now is the Big Picture.

Every successful business has a system with steps that are followed day in and day out. A business can't run without a system and step-by-step processes. Correction, a *profitable* business can't run without a system and step-by-step processes.

If something doesn't seem to be working properly in your business, then take a step back, look at the Big Picture, review these five steps, and find out where within these steps the problem is occurring. I guarantee the problem will fall under one of them.

You see, this business isn't rocket science. It is simple math and a simple system. Stop trying to re-create the wheel. Stop dwelling on the mistakes of your past. Stop invalidating this business like broke people do and start embracing the resources provided to you here in this book. Start implementing the tools I am giving you. Start asking questions and communicate with me and my best-in-the-country staff. Start experiencing the life that real estate investing can offer you – when done the correct way.

MARKETING YOUR BUSINESS

I've heard many people say over the years that they have been to this or that seminar, bought this or that course, and yet they still don't know where to start because they are so overwhelmed by all this information. Here is the answer to that problem: *Get your phone to ring!* Nothing else matters if you are not marketing your business in a way that allows you quickly to locate sellers and buyers. This is the most important step, so focus on this step first. Again, there is no sense in worrying about negotiating with sellers or structuring deals if you don't even have deals to work on.

One of the first hurdles of marketing your business is to learn not to be afraid to let people know your intentions. You want people to know what you do. Be proud that you are a real estate investor. With that said, lead-generation and marketing is an entire course itself; however, you only need a few simple techniques to jump-start finding motivated sellers and buyers. Keep it simple and cost-effective.

MY FAVORITE MARKETING TECHNIQUES

DIRECT MAIL

Use handwritten letters, postcards, business letters, etc., and the more personal-looking, the better. I find invitation-size envelopes with actual stamps and handwritten addresses get the best results. You want the letter to look like it is coming from a family member so it gets opened rather than quickly thrown in the trash.

QUICK TIP ABOUT DIRECT MAIL

Determine the type of deals that you are trying to pursue (short sale, seller finance, rehab, etc.) and mail to a list of people that fall in to your target categories. These days you can purchase mailing lists to target just about any group of people. Find a local list broker that you trust, explain who you are trying to reach with your mailings, and then start mailing. Direct mail is not difficult, but it is tedious, which is why most people don't do it. Good news for you is that when you do it, competition will be minimal. Also make sure that you test your mailings in small quantities (in the hundreds, not thousands).

TYPES OF SELLERS YOU SHOULD TARGET AND CONSIDER MAILING

- Pre-foreclosure

- Out-of-State Owners

- Free-and-Clear Owners

- Bankrupt Owners

- Divorce

- Job Loss

- Expired MLS Listings

- Landlord/Owners

- Junker Properties

- Medically Afflicted Owners

- Vacant Houses

DIRECT MAIL EXAMPLE 1

Dear

Hi My name is Brian Evans

My wife Danielle and I would like to

$ Buy $

your house at

Please call us at :

PH :

FAX :

EMAIL :

Please Call !

Thanks,

Brian

DIRECT MAIL EXAMPLE 2

SIGNAGE

It is very important for you to know that in most, if not all, areas of the country, the use of roadway signs are against the law. Use of signs could result in large fines or penalties. On the flip side, signs are cheap and they get your phone to ring very well. Consult with your attorney and ask your city to determine whether putting out lead generating signs will work for you.

BUYING-HOUSES SIGN EXAMPLE 1

BUYING-HOUSES SIGN EXAMPLE 2

QUICK TIP ABOUT BUYING-HOUSES SIGNS

If you do get your attorney's blessing, then here are a few tricks: The brighter and uglier the better. No sentences, just a big heading and a phone number. Signs can be nailed or zip-tied to telephone poles or staked in the ground at busy intersections. If you do put out signs, make sure that the phone number you use goes to a voice mail box, or voice answering service, not to you personally. Put the signs up as high as possible so they will stay up longer. Lastly, hire someone to put out your signs.

SELLING-HOUSES SIGN EXAMPLE 1

SELLING-HOUSES SIGN EXAMPLE 2

SELLING-HOUSES SIGN EXAMPLE 3

SELLING-HOUSES SIGN EXAMPLE 4

QUICK TIP ABOUT SELLING-HOUSES SIGNS

Notice anything different about the signs I use to find buyers for my houses? Yes, they are ugly. Who in their right mind would call this person, let alone buy or lease a house from him? The answer is: everyone. Ugly handwritten signs are meant to do two very important things: (1) Get noticed and (2) get the phone to ring. Trust me, you will get more calls with signs like these than you will with professionally printed signs –guaranteed. Plus, this type of marketing is more cost-effective, and you have more flexibility with your messages.

NEWSPAPER ADS

Place ads in the investment property section if you are looking for sellers, or in the homes for sale section if you are looking for buyers. If you plan to run ads regularly, then you are better off to go ahead and pay for every day of the week because you will probably get more calls during the week than the weekend.

NEWSPAPER AD EXAMPLES FOR BUYING HOUSES

WE BUY HOUSES - CASH
Any Area - Any Condition
555-555-1234

WE BUY HOUSES
FAST!
555-555-1234

STOP FORECLOSURE
555-555-1234
www.example.com

BRIAN BUYS HOUSES
Quick Closings
555-555-1234

Behind on Payments?
Call Brian
555-555-1234

WARNING
Call Me First!
I Buy Houses - Cash
555-555-1234

AVOID FORECLOSURE
Free Report!
24 hr: 555-555-1234

When taking calls from sellers I would strongly advise you not to take these calls personally, ever! Have the calls forwarded to a live operator.

BRIAN'S ULTIMATE RESOURCE

I use Pat Live in my business and would strongly encourage you to use it, too. Pat Live employs your script with all callers and answers the phone 24/7 so a call will never be missed. Additionally, you can have these calls go to a voice mailbox where you ask callers to leave their name, phone, and property address and you'll call them back immediately. To try this great service go to:

www.PatLive.com/signup/brianevans

NEWSPAPER AD EXAMPLES FOR SELLING HOUSES

MUST SELL BY 8/15
CHEAP - CASH
Worth $110k Asking $72k
123 Main St
Call: 555-555-1234

Nice Foreclosure Homes
Buy Cheap Equity Now!
Call: 555-555-1234
www.example.com

INVESTOR SPECIAL
Must Sell By 6/15
Worth $79k Asking $47k
Call: 555-555-1234

HANDYMAN SPECIAL
No Bank Needed
Lease to Own
24 Hr: 555-555-1234
www.example.com

NO BANKS NEEDED
Owner Finance
Lease to Own
24 Hr: 555-555-1234
www.example.com

When taking calls from buyers, I find that it is best to have the calls go to a 24-hour voice mailbox with options to hear property info, including directions, on the homes you have available, answers to frequently asked questions, and instructions on what the caller should do next. Taking calls directly and repeating information for buyers will get old very quickly and burn you out. This is not the best use of your time.

QUICK TIP ABOUT NEWSPAPER ADS

To get the best response from your ads, make sure that you also purchase white space (a blank line) above and below the text of your ad. Ads bordered with white space pop out and stand out from the other ads. Don't ever put an ad in the newspaper without doing this.

BRIAN'S KEY POINT

Once you create a system for getting your phone to ring, everything else will fall into place.

ADDITIONAL METHODS TO FIND DEALS

If your marketing budget is limited, then you will have to be more aggressive on the front end until you can close some deals to better fund your marketing. What this means is that you are going to have to pick up the phone and start dialing for dollars. If you don't have the marketing money, you need to get your phone to ring, then you will have to pick up the phone and make sellers' phones ring. Either way, in order to find deals, someone's phone must be ringing. Here are additional cost-effective methods you should consider in order to find deals:

- Look for motivated sellers and/or distressed houses online:

  □ www.fsbo.com

  □ www.craigslist.org

  □ Real-estate-owned (REO) sites

  □ Foreclosure sites

- Look for For Sale by Owner (FSBO) ads in the newspaper.

- Drive around looking for FSBO signs in front of houses.

- Drive around looking for vacant or abandoned houses. Trust me, you will know if the house is vacant (tall grass, unkept, trash, peeling paint, broken windows, rotten wood, bad roofs, bad smells, boarded up, piles of phone books on front step, etc.). Once you have located a vacant house, you need to find the owner. Ask the neighbors if they know how to get in touch with the owner. Look on tax rolls. Use a skip-trace service like www.findtheseller.com.

- Work with Realtors. Develop good relationships with Realtors and ask them to help you search the multiple listing service (MLS) for deals based on criteria that you give them (discussed in more detail in a later chapter).

- Go to Real Estate Investor Association (REIA) meetings in your area and network with other investors. There can be good deals here from wholesalers, but make sure that you do your own due diligence on properties presented to you.

- Go to auctions or look on auction Web sites such as www.auction.com.

- Consider wrapping your vehicle in big bold letters saying, "I Buy Houses" and your phone number. This takes some guts, but it will get your phone to ring.

- Get an apprentice to help you implement your marketing to generate leads. Put the word out and advertise on free Web sites like Craigslist. Your ad should say "Real estate investor looking for apprentice." The sooner you start delegating tasks, the faster your business will grow.

- Find house scouts, who are, basically, people looking to make a little extra cash on the side by helping you find houses to buy. Ask them to drive around looking for FSBOs, vacant houses, etc., in specific areas that you tell them. Demand, at minimum, pictures of each house visited, a description of repairs needed, and the address. You will pay the house scouts based on each potential deal that they bring you as a result of their searching (as long as your criteria is met).

BRIAN'S ULTIMATE RESOURCE

For a complete resource of information on how to find deals and make more money in real estate than you ever imagined possible go to www.FreeMakeMoneyGift.com and sign up for a free test drive.

UNDERSTAND YOUR MARKET

I believe, as a real estate investor, that it is very important to understand your market. This doesn't mean that you have to be an expert and know every little detail about your area, but it does mean that you should have a strong understanding of your market. The more you understand about the market where you invest, the more confident you will be in the investment decisions that you make. With a strong knowledge base, you will be better able to determine whether you want to hold or flip a property based on the various area conditions in your market.

I would recommend devoting an hour out of your day once each week in order to develop a strong understanding of the market you are investing in. Some of the statistics I would recommend you look at are:

- Population

- Area growth rate

- Area median income

- Area education level

- What are the primary industries?

- Is the market growing or shrinking?

- Where are the high-end properties?

- Where are the low-end properties?

- Where are the jobs?

- Where are the best shopping and entertainment centers?

- Which areas are suffering from high turnover?

- Are new transportation corridors in the offing?

- What are the absorption rates for commercial and residential areas?

- Where is the overall national economy on its gravitational cycle?

- What effect is the current global market having on jobs, land, and the overall economy?

- How does the area compare, statistically, to other areas of similar size?

Many market-related statistics are available from the U.S. Census Bureau, area Chambers of Commerce, real estate professionals, banks and lenders, tax rolls, industry publications, and Web sites.

WEB SITES THAT WOULD BE BENEFICIAL FOR YOU TO CHECK OUT

- www.city-data.com

- www.census.gov

- www.trulia.com

- www.hud.gov

- www.uscounties.com

- www.naco.gov

- www.haines.com

- www.homeinfomax.com

- www.loopnet.com

ALWAYS FOCUS ON REVENUE

One of the most important things ever taught to me as an entrepreneur and a real estate investor is: You must *always focus on revenue*. I am going to restate this from time to time, so remember it as AFR.

Gosh, I can't stress enough how important this is for your real estate investing business, and every business for that matter. As a business owner, you are in business for one reason and one reason only: to make money. Lots and lots of money. Even nonprofit businesses have to make money in order to stay in business, so don't be fooled by the nonprofit part of it.

As a real estate investor, I know what it is like to be wondering when the next deal is going to take place and provide you with some cash in the bank. Maintaining business cash flow is one of the biggest hurdles in this business. Although it seems so simple to think that you should always focus on revenue, you'd be surprised how easy it is to lose this mindset. Nowadays, people (and I am guilty, too) get so caught up in the little day-to-day distractions like e-mail, phone calls, faxes, etc., that they forget to prioritize and focus on the task that will help to bring in the next paycheck.

THREE PRIMARY HABITS YOU NEED TO IMPLEMENT

There are three primary habits that you must implement as soon as possible to help you grow your business so that you can AFR.

1. Delegate tasks as often as possible: If you are the only one in your business, then this will be difficult but not impossible to implement. Ask yourself, is it time to hire help? At minimum, you may want to consider finding part-time assistance or an apprentice. However, I firmly believe that if you can't make money in this business by yourself, then you probably can't make money in this business when you have help. Close at least one deal before thinking about hiring help.

2. Prioritize your tasks and time appropriately: The first thing you do in the morning should not be to check your e-mail. It should be to create your to-do list for the day and do the most important things first that will allow you to get closer

to the next payday. Only after you complete your important tasks should you check your e-mails. Being busy and being productive are two very different things.

3. Create systems: Having systems in place is so important to the efficiency, longevity, and profitability of your business. The better systemized and organized you are, the easier it will be for you to AFR.

If I were you, I would create a Word document, center and bold the text, and type on the page "Always Focus on Revenue." Then enlarge the text as big as possible keeping all of the words on the page. Print the page and tape it in front of your desk so that you can see it every day.

If you are not the one focusing on revenue, then who is? Someone better be – otherwise you will end up another small-business failure statistic, and I do not want that to happen to you.

WHY INVESTORS GET A BAD RAP

Investors get a bad rap because most investors lack professional credibility. This issue is one of the most critical you may ever face, because it is something that is both constantly under scrutiny and something that is also fairly easy to develop – once you know exactly what you need to do.

What is credibility? One could easily apply a very broad definition, and thus simply assume it to be related to believability. I think a little more depth is necessary to get at the importance of this issue, so with a little help from our friends at Wikipedia, I can describe credibility as: "The objective and subjective components of the believability of a source or message. Traditionally, credibility is composed of two primary dimensions: trustworthiness and expertise, which have both objective and subjective components."

Let's take a closer look at this definition and simplify it. Credibility, fundamentally, has to do with the quality of a message, and that message has everything to do with your credibility as a real estate investor. Whether it's a marketing message, how you express yourself over the phone, and especially how you come across in person, the quality of your message has everything to do with your perceived credibility.

As previously alluded to, the other factor that ties in so critically to credibility is knowledge and expertise. Don't confuse experience with expertise, because they are two different things. Experience has more to do with time, while expertise can be achieved much more quickly.

As you will see in a few chapters, the best way to establish the expertise component of your business is through education and then applying it through experience.

The last feature of the definition of credibility to point out is the reference to both objective and subjective components. Your trustworthiness and expertise can be evaluated both objectively and subjectively, and it's important not to underestimate the value of either. For example, a client could find you subjectively credible (i.e., he or she has a good impression of you or feeling about you) but, if you don't back up what you say, the objective side of trustworthiness will come back to haunt you. That's why it's important to act out and achieve results rather than just talking a good game.

Similarly, one could subjectively present a good level of expertise by communicating with industry jargon and relying on client ignorance to get ahead. This may work for a select few, but the expertise you present can and needs to be backed by real knowledge to create sustained levels of success. I have heard a few pundits out there say things like, "Fake it 'til you make it." But I find this to be a slippery slope that can cause permanent damage to your business if you aren't making the proper effort to really learn what you are doing. If you think education is expensive, try ignorance. A better quote is, "Be real, every deal." Your customers will, at some point, come up with an objective assessment of your expertise, and in the absence of real knowledge, you might find yourself in trouble. Education and evaluated experience are the keys to true knowledge and expertise that you can back up. With that said, let's move on.

To better understand the psychological nature of real estate investing, you first need to understand the nuances of the real estate market and how the opinion of the market differs between investors and the rest of the universe. Consumers might use the following terms or phrases to describe the current real estate market:

- Bleak

- Dismal

- Sluggish

- A bubble that has burst

- Catastrophic

Investors, on the other hand, might use a slightly different set of descriptions for the exact same real estate market, because we will always view market conditions different from the majority, instead saying:

- Opportunistic

- A rare gem of possibility

- A millionaire-maker

- Ripe for the picking

- A never-ending opportunity

Perhaps you can see where I'm going with this. The truth for investors is that there has rarely been a market condition that is better than the one you are experiencing right now. Like the 100-year flood, you may never see the likes of this again in your business lifetime and it represents a rare and exciting opportunity for people like us. The public, influenced as you know by popular media see things differently and in a much more pessimistic light. As a real estate investor, you have an amazing opportunity in front of you and in the spirit of building a multimillion-dollar business you also have to bear in mind that your view of the market is dramatically different from the one your clients will have. This is a gap that needs to be bridged if you are to have optimal success.

In part because of the difference in perception about the market and in part for reasons I'm about to describe, it is the unfortunate truth that investors, as a group, often get a bit of a bad rap and have a questionable reputation in the world of real estate. Why is that? I can think of several reasons worth discussing:

- Greed

- Jealousy

- Ignorance

- Dishonest

- Lack of credibility

Let's take a moment and further explore each of these issues. First, you have the greed factor. In a nutshell, what I'm referring to is the small percentage of real estate investors who let their pursuit of power, money, and glory (in no particular order) get in the way of running an ethical business. Ultimately, the emphasis should be on creating outcomes that benefit all parties. We've all come across examples of greed in this business, and if you haven't, you will. You can find it with the slumlord who maintains slovenly apartments to better line his or her pockets, as the scam artist who dupes others into sinking funds into phantom projects that never materialize, or as the heartless person who promises the world to a client in pre-foreclosure only to leave them stranded at the eleventh hour. I could go on and on.

These select few who make a bad name for the rest of us are an unfortunate reality for those of us who wish to run our business the right way. There's not much you or I can do about it. Real estate is a commodity for which tremendous profits can be realized, and as a result, some greedy people are going to get in the mix. What you can do is recognize how these people affect the reputation of real estate investing as a business and place extra emphasis on building a reputable business that will show the true colors of your craft.

Second, you have the issue of jealousy. I might be sparking a little controversy here, but part of the current reputation for real estate investing as a profession comes from real estate agents and brokers. It is unfortunate, but some (not all) of your real estate colleagues are often working against you either consciously or subconsciously. If these select few would simply take the time to learn something new and open their eyes to the many unconventional and creative opportunities that real estate offers, then they could truly understand why you choose to be a real estate investor rather than a real estate agent. There are hundreds of differences between selling houses for a commission and buying and selling houses for equity and profit. Personally, I'll take the equity and profit any day of the week.

Is this reason for real estate investors to be alarmed? Not necessarily. Rather, it is important to be aware of what preconceptions exist for those in the business. You must build your business in spite of these obstacles rather than simply expecting for things you can't control to somehow change.

Third, you have the issue of ignorance, not so much on the part of your colleagues but on the part of the general public. Let me explain that I'm not suggesting the public is ignorant in a general sense. What I am suggesting, though, is that the general public is very unlikely to be up to speed with the concepts and techniques that you will be utilizing as a real estate investor. For example, the majority of homeowners buy and sell only a few homes in their lifetimes and, in doing so, utilize Realtors who are pretty much driving the transactions based on conventional wisdom. We as investors, on the other hand, are trained to buy and sell properties as a business with perhaps dozens if not hundreds of completed deals. That said, while this type of ignorance may affect the reputation of investing as a profession, it also opens a door of opportunity for you to establish a local name for yourself and your business that will literally make believers out of your clients.

Next is the unfortunate issue of a few dishonest investors out there who threaten what you do on a daily basis. Whether it is an unscrupulous rehabber who cuts corners or abandons a project, or a foreclosure investor who skims equity or takes funds up front from clients only to disappear, the bottom line is the same. Like any industry, real estate has its share of bad apples who, unfortunately, get more attention than us good apples. The media loves a story with an evil investor scamming an innocent consumer simply because (a) it's negative, and (b) people pay attention to that kind of stuff. My commentary on the media aside, it is important that you recognize what your clients may be hearing or reading and how that relates to what you do for a living. Don't let yourself get defensive, but understand that your reputation will in part be built upon showing clients that you do not fall into the bad apple category.

Last on my list of things that give investors a poor reputation is a simple lack of true knowledge and professionalism. In short, some of your colleagues just don't know what they are doing, and this can affect the overall perception of what you do as a business. While I cannot oversee a proper education for every investor, I think – in fact, I know – that this can work to your advantage. Where other investors fall short, you will finish. Where other investors are weak, you will be strong. Business is about survival of the fittest, and even though some investors may damage the reputation of the business as a whole by not being very good at what they do, that can and should be seen as a great opportunity to establish your own reputable foundation and build from it.

BRIAN'S JOURNAL ENTRY

"My Early Days As a Real Estate Investor"

It is interesting for me to think back about my early days as a real estate investor. When I finally made the decision that I wanted to make a living buying and selling real estate, I was filled with mixed emotions of excitement and fear. However, I knew deep down in my heart and soul that this was right and that I was going to succeed no matter what obstacles I encountered and no matter how long it would take. It is definitely easier for me to say this now, however I won't lie, there were times when I second-guessed myself and picked up the newspaper, skimming the employment section "just in case."

My journey to becoming a successful real estate investor was without question the most difficult thing I have ever set out to do in my life, and yet this has also been the most fulfilling and personally gratifying journey I've ever experienced to date. There were many nights of sleeplessness and anxiety (and still are on occasion), however I realize now that every experience, positive and negative, was and is meant to be.

I went from a college graduate, to an insurance underwriter on Wall Street, to a failed retail coffee shop owner, to a real estate investing novice, to a millionaire real estate investing expert, to an author and a real estate investor coach. This was all over a six-year period, and I have to be honest, I wouldn't change the past for anything. I loved the business of real estate investing before I could fully comprehend what it was all about and I love it now even more. Real estate is the greatest wealth-generating vehicle on the planet, and I'm proud to be a figure within the industry.

BRIAN'S KEY POINT

If you want people to believe in the message that you are saying, they must first believe in you.

Therefore, if you want people to believe in you, you must express trustworthiness, knowledge, and expertise. It's one thing to be trustworthy and do a good job of convincing a client that you are as advertised. Not to be a cynic here, but any good salesperson can convey a level of trustworthiness and I've seen both consumers and other investors alike burned by the real estate investor who was high on sales skills and low on ethics. In my opinion, there is no such thing as business ethics, only ethics in general.

Do you ever feel like you're missing something and that something must be slipping through the cracks and keeping you from reaching your full potential? Chances are, this missing element may be basic real estate knowledge. If you're like me, you weren't born a real estate investor. Perhaps you just started this business recently. Whatever your particular situation, there are some tricks of the trade that will help you move faster along that proverbial learning curve to reach greater levels of success. If you could learn to be more efficient at tapping into your own potential and, in doing so, become more successful, how many additional doors of opportunity do you think may begin to swing open in your business and in your life?

Trustworthiness is best demonstrated by results. In short, do what you say and say what you do. It may sound like an oversimplification, but it does carry a lot of weight and can go a long way toward establishing the trustworthiness component that your business will need to be successful.

DO WHAT YOU SAY

"Do what you say," sounds simple and miniscule, doesn't it? Well, it is far from it. How many times has someone told you that he would call you back, get back to you about something, keep you in the loop, let you know, shoot you an e-mail, or whatever, and nothing happened? Better yet, how many times have you said that to someone and then not followed through with what you said?

Of all the pet peeves that I have, this one might top the chart. There is nothing more annoying than people who say they will do something and then don't do it! And 90% of the time, I would guess that they knew when they said it that they weren't going to do anything – but they just said it anyway. Why? Because they didn't want to hurt my feelings or let me know up front and were hoping I would just forget about it. It makes no sense, does it?

Confession time. I was once guilty of this habit. And that is exactly what it is, by the way, a *bad* habit. In my early investing days, I can recall times when I said that I would call back a seller or buyer and then didn't. Why did I do this? I think, at the time, it was just the easy way out, easier, that is, to say it to not disappoint the other person. Well, eventually, I was called out on it, and I was embarrassed. From then on, I committed myself to always do what I say I would, and on the flip side of that, always hold people accountable to what they say. Funny thing is, once you make this commitment, you will be surprised how many other people don't do what they say.

Although breaking this bad habit wasn't easy, once I committed myself to breaking it, it wasn't long before I was always doing what I said I was going to do. Am I perfect now? Absolutely not, but I guarantee that I am better than 99% of other real estate investors and business professionals out there when it comes to doing what you say.

THERE ARE TWO SECRETS TO MAKING THIS WORK FOR YOU:

Secret 1: Don't say you'll do something if you are at all unsure that you'll be able to do what you say.

Secret 2: Use a Daily Planner.

Use a Daily Planner you say? How is that such a big and all-important secret? Well, I will tell you that once I implemented and committed myself to using a Day Planner in my business and life, not only was I able to keep my promises with ease but also keep other people accountable with ease.

I'm not talking about an electronic planner, a BlackBerry or Microsoft Outlook. I'm talking about a good old-fashioned leather planner with a paper and pen. There is absolutely nothing better – guaranteed.

Every day when I get to my office, the first thing I do is open my Planner and place it in a stand on my desk so that I can see my schedule and to-dos. If there are any to-dos from the day before that I didn't complete, then I immediately write them down on that day's page so that I am reminded to get them done.

You see, my planner is my excuse to forget. I have a terrible memory, just ask my wife. However, because I have established such a good habit of using and implementing my planner every day, it has allowed me to be a better businessperson and appear to have the memory of an elephant.

Not only this, but my Planner is my "idea center." If you are an entrepreneur like me, then you probably have tons of new and great ideas on a regular basis about how to make big bucks in real estate or any other business venture. The thing about me is that I write these ideas down in my Planner, and then once they are in my planner the idea has a much better chance of being implemented.

If you are not using a good old-fashioned Planner to organize yourself in your business and life, then it's likely that you will struggle to keep your commitments and hold other people accountable to their commitments, no matter how big or small these commitments are.

I am a firm believer that the more organized and systemized you get, the faster your business will grow and the more money you will make. Your Planner is your secret weapon, your friend, your memory box, your idea center, your accountability partner, your implementation device.

Put it this way, if there was ever a fire and I only had a second to grab something and run, you would see my laptop in one hand and my Planner in the other. It is invaluable to me as a business owner and entrepreneur.

BRIAN'S ULTIMATE RESOURCE

If you have ever found yourself unorganized, unfocused, unable to prioritize, etc. then this very well could be the most beneficial resource recommendation of your life! If you want to use the exact same planner that I use and have been using for years then go to www.q4systems.com.

DON'T BE AFRAID TO ANNOY PEOPLE

As a real estate investor, you will undoubtedly annoy people on occasion as a result of your marketing. When you mail letters and postcards, put up signs, etc., not everyone is going to like your message or even be happy that you contacted them. Some will ask to be removed from your list; others will not like your street signs. The key is not to let the negative, the haters, and the easily annoyed keep you from doing what you do. The fact is, some will, some won't, so what, someone's waiting (SW, SW, SW, SW).

Every week in my real estate investing business, I get a call from someone who has requested not to be contacted again (after the first letter). One time, someone even took his complaint to the attorney general's office. Can you believe that? All because I sent a handwritten letter in the mail saying that I wanted to buy his house. It's called marketing, buddy. If you are not interested in selling your home, then here's an idea, don't call. The attorney general's office really seemed like it could not care less about this complaint. There is no law about mailing letters to generate business. The unfortunate thing is that the complainant apparently had such a pathetic life that he let one little letter in the mail upset him so much that rather than throwing it away he felt the need to retaliate. Again, my reaction to this is, oh well, too bad for him. I didn't do anything wrong, so back to running my business.

To be successful in this business, you need to very quickly whack the suspects and only work with the prospects. You must not be afraid to annoy people with your marketing. Don't let the people who get annoyed by your marketing efforts scare you away from this business. Your marketing is the heart that pumps blood into your business. If you turn that off, then everything else will go dark.

BE A FIGHTER PILOT

There are many factors that go into becoming a massively successful real estate investor, and there is one profession in particular I believe offers an appropriate comparison to the overall skills you need to have in this business, albeit on a slightly different playing field. This comparable profession is that of a fighter pilot. Let me explain. Fighter pilots are the absolute best at what they do. They must go through rigorous tests and training before they get their wings. Not everyone who sets out to become a fighter pilot reaches his or her goal, because it takes a certain kind of individual to overcome the challenges and develop the skills required before the military hands over the keys to a multimillion-dollar aircraft.

Here is a brief list of some of the skills I think are shared between a fighter pilot and a real estate investor:

- Desire to be the best at what they do

- Willingness to work hard under all circumstances

- Ability to handle pressure very well

- Ability to think and make decisions very quickly

- A love for speed and results

- Having a very strong understanding of the business/aircraft that they are operating

- Commitment to serve their business/country

- Always striving to make their skills better

- Have trust in their mentor/wingman

- Display a very high level of personal confidence

Obviously, these are not all of the comparisons that could be made between a fighter pilot and a real estate investor. In fact, there are probably hundreds of comparisons that could be made. It is fun though, isn't it? If you can think of any more comparisons, then I would love to read them. Just send me a fax, 859-201-1441, and I just might include them in a second edition down the road.

Here is one more thing to consider when comparing yourself as a real estate investor to a fighter pilot. Your workspace (your desk, office, etc.) should be very structured and organized, similar to the fighter pilot's cockpit. When you are working at your desk, in order to be most efficient and effective without loss of momentum and concentration, you need to have everything near you so that you can work quickly. You should know where the things are that help you work effectively and have them within reach. When you are in your cockpit, you should become focused on accomplishing your goals and tasks that are in front of you. Prioritize your mission for each day and work down the list from most important to least important. You should always be focusing the most effort on the deal that is closest to cash and getting you paid. Always keep this and other similar deals on your radar.

What I would like to do now is have you complete a short exercise. This simple questionnaire is based on an honest rating of yourself and (if you have one) your current real estate investing business. You may score high in certain areas but not in others. That's OK. I'll have you complete the same questionnaire at the end of the book so you can measure your progress after learning what I have to teach. So, let's get started.

QUESTIONNAIRE (ROUND 1)

On a scale of 1 to 10, with 1 being the worst and 10 being the best, circle your answer:

I would rank my current understanding and use of a professional support team a:

1 2 3 4 5 6 7 8 9 10

I would rank my current level of real estate investment education a:

1 2 3 4 5 6 7 8 9 10

I would rank my positive attitude as a real estate investor a:

1 2 3 4 5 6 7 8 9 10

I would rank my current understanding of the necessary
skills as a real estate investor a:

1 2 3 4 5 6 7 8 9 10

I would rank my current passion for real estate investing a:

1 2 3 4 5 6 7 8 9 10

I would rank my current professional appearance as a real estate investor a:

1 2 3 4 5 6 7 8 9 10

I would rank my current office set-up for my real estate business a:

1 2 3 4 5 6 7 8 9 10

I would rank my current accumulation of credentials and
testimonials for my business a:

1 2 3 4 5 6 7 8 9 10

I would rank my current real estate transactional experience a:

1 2 3 4 5 6 7 8 9 10

I would rank my current understanding and use of a
professional business plan a:

1 2 3 4 5 6 7 8 9 10

I would rank my current marketing plan for my real estate business a:

1 2 3 4 5 6 7 8 9 10

I would rank my current understanding of and approach
to effective meetings a:

1 2 3 4 5 6 7 8 9 10

I would rank my current understanding and mastery of
real estate paperwork a:

1 2 3 4 5 6 7 8 9 10

I would rank my current understanding of and commitment to customer
service a:

1 2 3 4 5 6 7 8 9 10

I would rank my current tax/corporate structure for my
real estate business a:

1 2 3 4 5 6 7 8 9 10

I would rank my current understanding and pursuit of
private lending a:

1 2 3 4 5 6 7 8 9 10

I would rank my overall credibility as a real estate investor a:

1 2 3 4 5 6 7 8 9 10

Did you know that the statistics are not in your favor? By that I
mean it is accurately estimated that only 20% of readers will complete
the above survey and the other 80% will choose to skip it. If I were a
gambling man then I would wager that the 20% who do complete the
survey have slightly if not immensely larger bank accounts than the

80% who choose to skip it. The choice is yours. I'll wait if you want to go back and complete the self-evaluation questionnaire!

The remainder of this book, as you will see, addresses the things that will help start, maintain, and grow rapidly your real estate investing business. You will easily identify with some of the topics I address while others will take effort to learn. Each chapter addresses a different building block that is relevant to your success and longevity as a real estate investor. So stick with me, and let's continue this exciting and informative journey to your ultimate real estate investing success.

CHAPTER 2

The Professional Support Team of an Ultimate Real Estate Investor

One of the first things you need to realize as a real estate investor is that you don't have to master all the skills of running a successful business on your own. Forget for a moment the image of the solitary and committed entrepreneur, however nostalgic it may seem. Every great entrepreneur in history had a good support team even if that team didn't get all the credit in the end. Why should you be any different? I have confidence that everyone has the potential for greatness, and step one in reaching that milestone is acknowledging that you're not alone.

Your professional team is essential to the flow, success, and longevity of your business. After all, your clients – both present and future – won't expect you to have all the answers and won't expect you to be able to do everything even if you don't realize that just yet. I will say this, though, and forgive me if I repeat it later: It's OK to say, "I don't know," so long as you mention that you know where to find the answer. Stated another way, it's far better to defer a question from a client to a team member rather than just make up an answer because you're afraid to say, "I don't know." Deals fall apart when such things happen, so don't let that happen to you.

For starters, let's establish the framework for your professional team and then talk about the numerous attributes of having one. Depending on where you may have received some of your real estate education, you may see a team referred to as a "wealth team" or "power team," and I'm talking about the same thing here. Your team is the assembly of professionals who handle the aspects of your business that you either (a) don't have the background or expertise to handle or (b) choose not to spend time working on yourself. Both rationales are valid, so the important thing is to establish a competent team.

So who should be on your team? There are a couple of ways to think about this, and how you do so depends on who you are and how your business is organized. For example, are you currently working on real estate investing as a part-time venture? If so, then having some core elements of a professional team will likely be sufficient to help you get started. If your business is a full-time endeavor, then your team assembly will likely be a more comprehensive undertaking. The team members I find essential for all real estate investors, even part-timers and those just getting started, are:

Your Ultimate Team
(Mind Map)

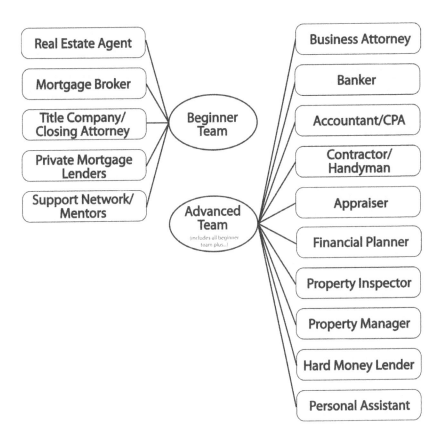

How's that for a list? Some of this will of course seem perfectly logical, and I don't want you to be daunted by this list if you're new to the business. This is part of what it means to be a real estate investor. Let's take a closer look at each team member and how they can dramatically help your business.

BRIAN'S KEY POINT

Make sure that you don't ever become dependent on any individual team member. When you become dependent on someone, then you can become trapped within your business. Always have other alternatives to consider.

TEAM MEMBER 1: REAL ESTATE AGENT

Whether or not you regularly use the local multiple listing service (MLS) to find deals for your business, a good real estate agent (or agents) is still a critical part of your success. You are somewhat a reflection of what your team accomplishes behind the scenes, and a good realtor can do many things for you, including submission of offers and letters of intent to purchase, streamlining closings with either buyers or sellers, and helping you find buyers and, of course, deals. None of this requires having to spend a lot of your valuable time when you have the right agent on your team. This is a foundational team position that you need to take seriously.

BRIAN'S JOURNAL ENTRY

"How I Found My Number One Real Estate Agent"

Having the right or wrong real estate agent on your team could very well make or break your business in the early days as an investor. There came a time in my business when I felt the need to find a person to focus all of their time on finding buyers for my houses so I could focus more of my time on buying more. Previously I had tried to hire someone on a commission basis to handle this, however either my lack of attention to their actions or the persons' drive kept this from being a success. Subsequently, I casually tried to work with a real estate agent that was new to the business, however this didn't really work out either.

And then came Jane (names changed for privacy). I was in the process of flipping a property that I had just purchased on a short-sale transaction to a couple whose Realtor approached me from my For Sale By Owner ad in the yard. This transaction was somewhat complicated and frustrating, as most short-sale deals are, however Jane maintained her professionalism and follow-up throughout the entire process. She wasn't my Realtor, however she was a Realtor who was focused on getting things done to get the deal closed.

Shortly after this particular closing I decided to reach out to Jane and interview her about acting as my Realtor for the properties that I want to sell. She gladly accepted and it has been a win-win relationship ever since. The lesson I learned here was that I went out and found someone who was already good at what they did, who had good follow-up skills, who was hungry for more, and who understood what it takes to get paid based on results.

TEAM MEMBER 2: MORTGAGE BROKER

Another critical team member to find early on as a real estate investor is a mortgage broker. They can be instrumental in getting your buyers qualified, and allowing you to recognize profits in a more streamlined manner. Buyer qualification is one of the tough issues in today's real estate market, and this team member alone can be hugely effective for you and your business.

Good collaboration with a reputable mortgage broker can help you find a foundation in the world of home finance. You don't need to be up to speed on all emerging trends, but what a good broker can offer you gives you information that you can pass along to your clients to establish you as a knowledgeable and credible investor.

TEAM MEMBER 3: REAL ESTATE BUSINESS ATTORNEY

A good real estate business attorney can help you review your paperwork to ensure it is compliant with local laws and can protect you sufficiently in the event of a dispute. Although it isn't pleasant to think about needing a real estate business attorney as part of your team, it is absolutely essential. In fact, you probably should have more than one from whom you can get advice. Unfortunately, this and so many other professions are so tied to lawsuits and other unsavory topics – and you want an attorney on your team for this exact reason. The chances of being sued, especially if you have a successful business, are pretty good, and you want to have a real estate business attorney who understands your business if that happens.

When choosing a real estate business attorney to handle the professional business matters that arise, my best advice is not to skimp or else you may be sorry you did one day. A good real estate business attorney also does a lot for your professional reputation. Being able to reference the fact that you have an attorney or need to run something by your attorney is not only a professional and credible approach but also discourages any potential clients with unscrupulous intentions from pursuing their objectives. The best value a good real estate business attorney can offer is to position you where you rarely, if ever, need them.

TEAM MEMBER 4: TITLE COMPANY/CLOSING ATTORNEY

One more critical team member is the person or organization that handles your closings. A title company (or closing attorney in some states) can add a layer of professionalism to your business by making the process seem simple with minimal issues. The performance of your title company can be a solid reflection of your business, so it is important to choose carefully and check qualifications for the variety of transactions you will be doing. Title companies also perform title searches, which can help you avoid unnecessary issues with transfers of ownership and recording of documents. I would also highly recommend that your closing attorney close your rental or lease option agreements. You can find no better witness if a tenant cries foul than your closing attorney. When in doubt, let your closing attorney do what they do best, which, in this case, is finalize agreements between two parties so that you can do what you do best, which is buy and sell houses.

TEAM MEMBER 5: BANKER

A good real estate investor should have numerous financing options at his or her disposal, and a local banker should be on your team to help with these options. Local bankers can usually issue loans that national lenders cannot and be more flexible with you as you accumulate more and more properties. From a financial standpoint, local bankers can also help boost your business presence through issuance of business credit lines and by showing that you are a player on the local scene. Being committed to developing business relationships with local lenders will only open doors for you and will help establish your business as a fixture in the local economy as well.

BRIAN'S KEY POINT

One word of caution however, I recommend only using banker-borrowed money for short-term transactions. Avoid getting a new mortgage each time you want to buy a house in your business. Personally guaranteed debt can be very dangerous!

TEAM MEMBER 6: ACCOUNTANT/CPA

As your business grows, so too will the complexity of your asset base and the tax implications of running a business and managing these assets. A good accountant, while perhaps not an immediate concern for the novice real estate investor, is a team member that will soon provide clear benefits to your operations. Beyond the basics, a good accountant can help you structure the finances of your business properly and, in doing so, potentially save you thousands of dollars in taxes.

BRIAN'S KEY POINT

Be careful not to become obsessed with cost control and deductions. As the business owner, your job is to always focus on revenue, while your CPA can focus on reducing your cut to Uncle Sam.

TEAM MEMBER 7: CONTRACTOR/HANDYMAN

I have seen far too many investors attempt to justify a deal by saying it is profitable if they do the work themselves. These investors end up spending twice as much time on a project than necessary, overdo the budget in the process, and ultimately watch the profits slowly erode. Some of us are handier than others, and sometimes I find that being handy can be a detriment to investors as it makes them more prone to take on projects that they should hire out to be completed. As for me, the last thing that I want to do is pick up a hammer. Remember, you are running a business first and foremost, and taking care of property maintenance should be something you look to move past ASAP. You'll thank me later.

BRIAN'S JOURNAL ENTRY

"One Thing I Am Not Is a Handyman"

As a man, I have to swallow my pride when I say that one thing I am not is a handyman. The closest that I have ever gotten to becoming handy is mowing a yard, replacing a light bulb, installing a ceiling fan, using a carpet cleaner, hanging some pictures, and painting some walls. Honestly, that is about it! This doesn't mean that I haven't tried to do other things; this just means that I've tried to do other things considered "handy" and, well, failed. But hey, that's what I have brothers-in-law for.

And just to prove it to you, this one example that sticks out in my mind justifies the fact that I just don't have a knack for being a handyman: One time, an air conditioner wasn't working in my house. I thought for sure I was going to have to get the unit replaced. When the guy came out to see what the problem was, it turns out that all I needed to do was to replace the air filter. It had become clogged, and the A/C unit froze. If that repair guy had really wanted to, he definitely could have pulled one over on me by telling me the unit needed to be replaced. Thank goodness for honest people.

So, long story short, I was embarrassed, the repair guy probably thinks I'm not much of a man, and my wife made fun of me. Oh well, at least it is cool in the house again. If this isn't proof that you don't need to be handy to be a successful real estate investor, then I don't know what is.

And yes, I will check the filter going forward.

Your time should be spent constantly learning and growing your business, and as a result, you will be seen as the person in charge, not a person who wears all the hats. Lastly, when using contractors and any other professionals for that matter, always be sure to pay them as soon as the work is completed.

BRIAN'S KEY POINT

When you pay people promptly, they are much more inclined to respond to future requests promptly and refer new business to you.

TEAM MEMBER 8: APPRAISER

Your real estate agent may have a good appraiser they know, as may your mortgage broker, but most experienced investors have an independent appraiser that they call their own. This profession is the conscience that drives many real estate decisions, helping you to determine whether a deal has enough potential to pursue. Your real estate appraiser is there to validate assessments on properties when needed. Be aware that sellers tend to see more value in their properties than you do, so an appraiser can help give you the confidence to do your own due diligence to understand a property's real value. When in doubt, get an appraisal; however, don't automatically assume that this value is final. If you think a second appraisal is justified, budget accordingly.

BRIAN'S KEY POINT

An appraisal is only one other person's opinion. The true value of a property is what a buyer is willing to pay.

TEAM MEMBER 9: FINANCIAL PLANNER

Now that you are in business (or at least considering it), do you think it will change your financial outlook? You certainly hope that it will, and you should be prepared for the changes that are coming. A good financial planner is an essential part of modern money management, and you may want to have such a professional behind the scenes to help streamline and optimize your financial growth. Are financial planners critical to negotiating deals on properties? No. Are they critical to you feeling comfortable that you are operating with a defined plan that actually has a chart and a course? Absolutely. When you have confidence in the big picture of what your business is doing, you will be more confident and that will show in how you handle yourself and as you meet new people.

As a spin-off to this topic, you may also want to look into including a self-directed Roth IRA in your plan for retirement. Imagine buying and selling a property and the proceeds from that sale going directly to your self-directed Roth IRA, meaning you'll never have to pay tax on that money (when you follow the guidelines). This may sound too good to be true, but trust me, it isn't. If you haven't already, you should look into setting up a Roth IRA now while the government still allows you to and then converting it to a self directed Roth IRA down the road when you are ready. A qualified financial planner who has experience in self-directed Roth IRAs should be able to help you with this, but also do your own due diligence.

BRIAN'S ULTIMATE RESOURCE

For more information on self-directed Roth IRAs, visit www.trustetc.com and say that I referred you.

BRIAN'S JOURNAL ENTRY

"My First Deal in a Self-Directed Roth IRA"

When I first learned about self-directed Roth IRAs, I was totally amazed for two reasons: (1) Because I could essentially do deals within my Roth and the profit would be tax-free for life, and I was in control! And (2) because no one really knew about it, not attorneys, financial planners, or most affluent people I knew.

The first deal that I ever did in my self-directed Roth IRA took my account from $1,000 to $18,000 and change. That's right, I put more than $17,000 in profits from a house I flipped into my Roth IRA – tax free for life! Without making it too confusing for you, essentially my Roth IRA had an option to purchase a contract on a property. I found a new buyer who wanted the same property for more than my option to purchase price. I gave both agreements to my closing attorney and said make it happen, and the difference between my purchase price and my sales price was wired to my Roth IRA custodian as a tax-free investment profit for my Roth IRA. It's magical.

You don't get that kind of return in the stock market, that's for sure.

TEAM MEMBER 10: PROPERTY INSPECTOR

A dedicated property inspector is not necessarily a foundational team member for your real estate business, but the position is important especially as you start purchasing properties that you intend to keep for a while in order to produce a monthly income. The presence of a property inspector on your team helps you avoid problem properties (you know, the money pits out there) but also demonstrates to others that you are serious about your purchases and are ready to perform due diligence before ever completing a transaction.

The best way to find a good inspector is through a referral. Try to find an inspector who can also provide you with or knows someone who can provide you with certified termite inspections and mold inspections. These two little hidden demons can cause you serious problems down the road if you don't take the appropriate precautions. Take it from me – I have the financial scars to prove it.

BRIAN'S JOURNAL ENTRY

"My First Mold Encounter"

I bought a property "subject to" the existing mortgage. This is where you get ownership of a house and leave the debt on the property in place and make the monthly payments on the debt-holder's mortgage. Yes, this is a very creative method of buying properties, and one you should become familiar with as you grow your skills as an investor.

In any event, I bought this home, put a lease-option tenant in the property only to find out that the tenant was complaining of mold. I knew that this was one type of complaint not to drag my feet on, so I immediately had a mold remediation company go out to the house. Sure enough, there was a mold problem in the basement. Without hesitation, I had the mold removed within 24 hours and my bank account was about $7,000 lighter – ouch!

Lesson learned. When in doubt, get a property inspection (which should include a mold inspection) before closing on a property. In my attempt to save $250 on an inspection, I ended up losing $7,000 as a result. Not only that, but these same tenants never made their first month's payment, and I had to evict them. This house was doomed from the beginning; You can call this learning the hard way. I resolved the problems quickly, moved on quickly, and chalked it up as an unfortunate cost of doing business.

TEAM MEMBER 11: PROPERTY MANAGEMENT COMPANY

I learned a long time ago that property management is not a profession for the weak. Maybe many of you are very compassionate or generally tend to trust people you meet. These are redeeming qualities, yet they will make you a poor property manager. Managing tenants may not seem to be that big of a deal, but if you believe this, you have likely never had to coordinate a difficult eviction or deal with a "professional" tenant who likes nothing better than living rent free. In short, if you are serious about owning rental property, I believe property management is an essential part of your professional team. Pay someone else to deal with these problems while you utilize your time to invest in more deals.

Personally, I don't do straight rentals, but rather lease-options or seller financing, because I want my tenants to feel like homeowners. I want them having the feeling of home ownership in the property and maintaining or fixing up the place rather than trashing it. I find that if they have a vested interest in the home, it results in fewer problems. When problems do arise, the existence of property management in your world of real estate investing will save you countless hours, reduce stress, and boost your credibility by showing the world that you are running your business like a business and, in doing so, that you recognize your own limitations. Forget the investors you talk to who insist that managing your own properties is the only way to go. Most investors I have met who feel this way look like the business has aged them 15 years, and I don't think it's just a coincidence. Sometimes the best thing you can do is admit you need help with something. This is a great example of that point.

TEAM MEMBER 12: HARD-MONEY LENDER

A hard-money lender is a type of financier who specializes in properties that traditional lenders would often avoid, usually due to the condition of the property. The presence of a hard-money lender on your team validates you as a serious player in your market, because the hard-money lender allows you to pursue deals that other investors might walk away from and, therefore, allows you to reach more potential clients. In addition to allowing you to produce more revenue for your business, hard-money lenders also help refine your evaluation of potential deals. These financiers will fund only a certain percentage of the property's value, so this person can also help establish you as a better negotiator.

TEAM MEMBER 13: PRIVATE MORTGAGE LENDERS

This team member is quite different from the hard-money lender. More attention will be given to this subject in a later chapter, and it is worth mentioning here that sources of private money are a vital part of a real estate investor's team. Maybe you're one of the fortunate few who have plenty of your own capital to invest in your own business, but many investors (including myself when I got started) are lacking in this area and have to work to raise capital as a part of business development. Private mortgage lenders are vital to credibility for two key reasons.

First, if you can sell the concept of your investments and your business model to those who might provide you with funding, you can certainly sell it to your clients. Pursuit of private money gets you thinking differently about the upsides of your business, and this will make you more effective as both a salesperson and as a negotiator. Second, the ability to immediately produce capital to fund a particular deal gives you tremendous leverage, and this value cannot be overstated.

BRIAN'S JOURNAL ENTRY

"How I Got a Commitment
for $2M in Private Money"

It's true; I got a commitment for $2 million in private money from a regular individual just by asking. You think I'm crazy, I know, but it really isn't as difficult as you may think. Here's how I did it.

I was doing some thinking one morning about different ways that I could get more private money for my real estate deals. I decided to send out an e-mail to a list of other real estate investor/ wholesale buyers in my area. This is a list that I had personally accumulated over a period of about two years. Each time that I regularly advertised a house that I wanted to "wholesale" (sell quickly at a discount) to another rehab investor in my area, I would collect names, phone numbers, and e-mail addresses so I could quickly contact them for future deals. Rehab investors are always looking for new deals.

Anyway, at the time I had built a list of about 200 investors, so I decided to send an e-mail to them to see if I would get any responses. Here is exactly what my e-mail said:

"Hello, I have a very important question for you. Do you have an IRA or other investment capital not getting you a high rate of return safely? If so, please reply to this e-mail with your best contact number. I have some things you may want to consider. – Brian"

That was it. I got a few inquiries; after following up, one person said that he would be willing to lend up to $2 million. Sweet, huh? And all I had to do was ask. And there's no harm in asking, right?

TEAM MEMBER 14: ASSISTANT (LIVE OR VIRTUAL)

When businesses get busy, some sort of day-to-day help will inevitably be needed, and the process of bringing on an assistant can be critical to the ongoing success of your business. When you think about it, this is all about maximizing the time you can spend earning. Let's discuss both factors. First, there's the basic element of business productivity. You can only do so much yourself, and if the need to hire an assistant becomes real for you, then it probably is an indicator that things are going well enough to justify doing so. Believe me, you'll thank yourself in the end for doing it. There are various kinds of help that you can utilize. There is, of course, the person who helps with phone calls, filing, and knocking out things on the to-do list. There are also virtual assistants who handle things from afar and can be great for taking incoming calls, responding to e-mails, monitoring Web activity, and so on.

What choice in assistant you make is less important than the pure decision that one is necessary. At some point, your time will become too valuable to be doing the things an assistant can help with, not to mention having a staff will also bring valuable respect to your business by offering the appearance of a larger organization than may actually be the case. You don't have to create the image; people will perceive what they will and, if that gives you a boost, so be it. My suggestion is to look at this team member as a time saver and revenue builder first and foremost. If and when you do take the leap to bring on additional help, you'll wonder how you ever got by without it.

BRIAN'S KEY POINT

Do only what you do best and let someone else do the rest.

TEAM MEMBER 15: SUPPORT NETWORK/MENTORS

Last, but certainly not least, is your support network. You may be wondering what exactly I mean by this, and I'm ready to help lift the fog. Your support network is your friends and family who support what it is that you are doing as a real estate investor. Your support network also includes your colleagues, who are following similar paths to success and who equally appreciate the challenges and hurdles encountered along the way. It is vital to have some sort of support network and also important to recognize that it may not be composed principally of those closest to you. I have met many investors who have told me that, unfortunately, those closest to them are the ones that challenge or question why they were pursuing real estate. In the absence of a good professional support network, this kind of input can be, at a minimum, demoralizing and, in more extreme cases, prone to drive otherwise motivated investors right out of the business. Sound familiar?

The importance of a support network is not just to get pumped up and stay motivated. You should be able to fuel your own fire, at least to a certain extent, because that is just a part of being in business for yourself. Consider that professional athletes make the big bucks because they are the best at what they do and because they are self-motivated people. You need to strive to be the same way. That said, recognizing that external support is important is a critical part of being successful in business; you must get that support wherever you can find it. Maybe it is on the home front, and if so, then you're fortunate to have it. Maybe it's from a professional mentor, someone who chooses to take you under his or her wing to help you grow in your own business pursuits. Maybe it's a mastermind group of like-minded businesspeople who meet with some regularity to challenge one another and help fuel other members' successes. Any or all of these things are effective and powerful examples of a support network, so take this part of your professional team seriously and your business will reflect its presence.

BRIAN'S KEY POINT

There may be no better educational investment than the investment in a qualified mentor/coach to help you grow your business.

Now that we've covered the essential members of a professional team, let's wrap up this chapter by reviewing the importance of your team to the long-term success of your business. If you don't already, you should view yourself not as a CEO but as a CLO, chief leverage officer. Your professional team is depending on you to leverage their skills, which in turn creates a win-win relationship. First, a team expands your effective level of experience. Many investors find that a lack of experience is a drawback, especially when a client asks, "How long have you been doing this?" With a solid professional team, you as an investor can cite that your team has X years of experience, boosting your credibility without having to emphasize your own lack of experience.

Second, a professional team establishes an overall level of reliability by demonstrating that you have ready-to-go resources available to you. It adds a definite level of professionalism that suggests that paperwork will be reviewed by an attorney, that properties will be managed by a company dedicated to doing so, and that closings will be handled and managed by a licensed title company/closing attorney. Clients love the feeling that the situation is being handled professionally at each phase. I feel it looks better to have team members involved rather than presenting yourself as a one-stop shop. Informed clients will know better, and your team helps establish you as an authority figure in your market.

Like it or not, your clients (buyers and sellers) are your customers, and they need to trust what you do and want to do business with you. An investor who is able to delegate many parts of the purchase and sales processes to their team has the time to do what they do best: focus on the human side of the real estate business. Trust me, your clients will notice this level of attention to their needs and will see it as a validation of your reputation, and this will translate to more deals and more consistency for your business.

BRIAN'S ULTIMATE RESOURCE

I've developed a top-of-the-line support network to help you with all of your real estate needs. It's called Ultimate Real Estate Investors and you can learn more about this group and get an incredible free gift and test drive by visiting: www.UltimateRealEstateInvestors.com.

CHAPTER 3

The Education of an Ultimate Real Estate Investor

What do you think of when you hear the word "education"? Do you think of fundamentals like the ABCs? Do images of the hallowed halls of your alma mater come to mind instead? What about practical education? Did you need a certain degree or certification for your current profession? Any or all of these things are reasonable interpretations of what it means to be educated in today's society. That said, how does education apply to real estate?

Real estate investing, for as valuable a commodity as the product is, is a profession that doesn't require a degree to get started. When it comes to real estate interest rates, policy makers and the like will have finance backgrounds. Sure, some of your team members (CPAs and attorneys come to mind) have solid formal educations, but most were not trained in real estate-specific areas. What about realtors and mortgage brokers? Basically, it works like this: You take a training course over a few weekends, pass a test, and you're licensed either to broker real estate or issue mortgages. Not exactly the pinnacle of educational scrutiny, now is it?

Don't get me wrong. I'm not scoffing at the training certifications for these professions because you, as a real estate investor, need even less formal education to do what you do. There is no requisite certification or degree that stipulates you are able to invest in real estate. All you need is the desire, right? Oh, I wish it were that simple. If you think about it, part of the animosity faced by real estate investors from other professionals in the field may be due to just that. We're out there making offers and working deals (at least if we're doing what we're supposed to) without any sort of training. From the standpoint of the critics, it's just a step shy of real estate anarchy! I, of course, don't see it that way, though I do find it useful to see things from an alternative perspective from time to time.

Although informal, and absent professional credentials or certificates, education for the professional real estate investor is available and can take many forms. Many investors, to their credit and benefit, take advantage of several of the education options available to them. Some of the most common forms of real estate investor education include:

- Books and/or audio materials

- Attending meetings at a local Real Estate Investor Association (REIA)

- Seminars

- Personal coaching/mentoring

- Experience (aka the school of hard knocks)

Let's explore each of these options. Again, while no one educational outlet can ever promise to deliver everything you need to be successful, every little bit helps and adds to your arsenal of knowledge.

BOOKS AND/OR AUDIO MATERIALS

Never underestimate the power of a good read, and I have no doubt there is truth to this statement. As an investor, however, you must look at books (or the audio equivalents) as resources rather than your primary source of education. Let me be clear, books can provide you with:

- Basic real estate knowledge

- Inspiration

- A financial vocabulary

- An overview of real estate techniques

- Examples of how to interact with clients

The list could be longer, but my point here is that books are a basic resource, giving you so-called literacy in your craft. They may also be a source for inspiration. Perhaps it was a book that first gave you the idea to become a real estate investor. My selfish hope is that this book acts as your inspiration to achieve millionaire success and if so, that's great, because for me it was a book that originally sparked my intrigue with this business, too. What books cannot give you, however, are real-world experience. You can't substitute a book for going out, interacting with other investors, building a professional team, and simply working the business.

BRIAN'S JOURNAL ENTRY

"The Book That Got Me Interested in Real Estate Investing"

This is a fun little story that I enjoy telling people, because it goes to show you that little hinges swing big doors. By that I mean if one little book didn't come into my life, then I might not have become a real estate investor and you wouldn't have been able to read this eye-opening book as a result.

At the time, I was working in downtown New York City, and I had a pretty long commute to work, an hour and a half each way, to be exact. I had begun using this commute to do some reading to pass the time. Knowing this, my dad sent me a book in the mail one day, Retire Young Retire Rich by Robert Kiyosaki. On the cover there was a Post-it note that read, "Read this, take notes, let's talk. – Dad."

There was no, "I love you, Dad" or "How's things?" Just an ugly, yellow Post-it note. You see, my dad is all business, so this was not surprising to me, and since I'm his son, I couldn't let him down, so I immediately read the book.

The fact is, this book changed my thinking completely and went on to change the course of my life altogether. The main take-away message I got from the book was this: For most, life consists of making money to support your living, as well as saving money along the way so that you can eventually use that money to retire and stop working. Instead, your goal should be to do something that allows you to make a lot of money and grow wealth along the way so that you can retire (if you choose to) as early as possible.

The vehicle for wealth that resonated with me the most within the book was real estate investing. This new way of thinking sparked a thirst and craving for entrepreneurship and real estate that to this day has yet to slow down!

As you can see, one little book has the power to influence a change in the course of your life forever. I have seen many investors who had an impressive real estate library full of books, home study courses, and audio and video materials. Sure, it looks impressive, but the real validation of an ultimate real estate investor comes from actually doing deals. I'm in no way discouraging you from acquiring reading materials, as these will all help you educate yourself in some ways and build confidence in your ability to step out of your comfort zone to succeed.

What you want to avoid is the tendency to keep acquiring more books, looking for the proverbial magic bullet, when your fear of taking action is what is actually holding you back. This may not apply to you, but if it does, take a more rounded approach to your education, get out there, and start physically working the business. You will find it easier to cross that hurdle to success.

ATTEND MEETINGS AT A LOCAL REAL ESTATE INVESTOR ASSOCIATION (REIA)

One of the easiest and most cost-effective ways to educate yourself as a real estate investor is to attend local meetings with groups organized just for you. REIAs are very popular and widespread and can provide valuable information to you at a reasonable cost. The low cost and convenience of REIAs are two clear upsides. The downside is that the organizers dictate the topics that are presented and who does the presenting. You have little control over what and when you learn. You're not making that call. My suggestion is to use this as a component of your educational process and, especially if you want to get on the fast track to success, this should be only one of many learning opportunities for you.

Membership in a REIA gives you credibility, and not just from the education you will receive. You'll also have the wonderful opportunity to network with other investors and get your name circulating. These peers are people you may likely do business with in the foreseeable future. Wouldn't it be nice if they were already familiar with you?

SEMINARS

It seems like the real estate seminar concept has been just beaten to death at times, but be that as it may, it is still an educational outlet that produces countless successful investors each and every year. There can be life-changing value there despite the cynics who claim it is gimmicky or just a way to part otherwise decent people from their hard-earned money.

I have been around this business long enough to be familiar with most of the top seminar speakers out there, and I have compiled a brief checklist of things to consider when evaluating seminars as an educational opportunity. First, expect to pay more for seminar education. It will be more expensive than other types of education, so be aware of that up front and don't be one of those investors who expects something for nothing and walks away grumbling about the cost of the education, citing it as some sort of rip-off. Yes, some programs are better than others, but they will educate you and will usually do so in a shorter time frame than many of the other options you have.

Second, look for a company that has some diversity of training programs. Many seminar speakers like to home in on the hot topic of the day (e.g., auctions) and fail to educate their attendees with well-rounded fundamentals. Last, be ready to learn. Adults learn more slowly than young adults and need more repetition for things to stick. Therefore, the learning process can be tiring, especially if you still have a traditional job. Real estate doesn't have to be a full-time venture at first, but if seminars are your choice of education, be ready to spend some time at the training events and be ready to do what they tell you to do.

In almost every instance of seminar attendees being dissatisfied with the education they received, it really comes down to whether or not they did what they were taught to do. When and if you decide to invest your money in seminars, boot camps, books, tapes, CDs, DVDs, etc., always keep in mind that you are paying a premium for this information because it is information that could make you a lot of money. However, it will always be up to you to take the information you invested in and put it into action. Your investment in this information is worth nothing unless you act on it. So if you really don't have the time for this intensive style of education, that's fine. Choose something that fits your schedule and be OK with learning and growing your business more methodically. That's perfectly fine, especially if that's what best fits your current obligations and lifestyle.

Seminars are often comprehensive, giving you a crash course or a boot camp for real estate investing, accelerating your educational progress and quickly immersing you in the lingo you need to be familiar with. An investor attending a comprehensive seminar may pay more up front for their education, but it is usually highly focused and gives them the ability to almost instantly go out and start working like someone with more real-time experience. For the passionate beginner who wants to learn – and learn fast – this may be a great way to go, both to get educated and, by doing so, to get more confidence to go out immediately and start making things happen.

And in case you weren't aware, my friend and mentor Ron LeGrand, who wrote the foreword to this book, was once a broke car mechanic who borrowed $400 to go to his first real estate seminar. Now he flies around in a private jet. You do the math.

Seminars also put you in contact with a variety of potential colleagues who have goals similar to yours. Take advantage of this by exchanging business cards and making contacts for future reference and support.

PERSONAL COACHING/MENTORING

One of the single most valuable pieces of education you can get as an investor is to work one-on-one with someone who is more experienced than you, someone who has been there and done that. This can often be arranged for a fee. However, do not expect this to be inexpensive; remember, you are paying for someone's time and years of experience. With a personal coach or mentor, you can find special benefits like:

- Education from someone who makes a lot more money than you and lives a lifestyle that you are aspiring to have

- Education from someone who has experienced both success and failure

- Education in a one-on-one environment

- A chance to voice and discuss your own goals and interests

- A way to get all of your questions answered

- A way to learn at your own pace

Allow me to cut straight to the chase on this, because this is a topic not discussed enough. I firmly believe that you get to where you want to go 10 times or even a 100 times faster if you have a mentor, advisor, coach, etc., within your circle of influence. Everyone should have someone whom they can lean on and learn from to help them grow their business, their marketing, their self-esteem, their habits, and so on. Ninety-nine percent of the wealthiest people in the world have mentors, advisors, coaches (usually multiple mentors for that matter) that are in their circle of influence to make them better. And, did you know that even the mentors have mentors?

These types of people are always, and I mean always, trying to make themselves and their businesses better. This top 5-10% of the population doesn't ask how much it costs to acquire this new mentor, coach, advisor, information, etc., they ask how much it will make them. (If you zoned out on that last sentence, then read it again!)

So what does this have to do with you? Well, let me start by asking you, do you have anyone in your circle of influence that you consider to be a mentor, coach, advisor, confidant, etc.? If not, then why? If yes, why not more?

Think about it. If one new mentor could help give you the guidance, self-esteem, how-to information, marketing materials, explaining mistakes to avoid, etc., to make you and your real estate investing business better, wouldn't this be valuable to you? Of course it would. Knowledge helps you create income and wealth. Someone could always steal your wallet, but they can't steal what you know.

I know what you are saying, though. Getting a mentor, coach, or advisor will cost me money. Well, my response to that, which I learned from one of my mentors, is, "The price of education is cheap compared to the price of ignorance." Thanks Ron.

If my desire was to learn more about computers and software, I would do everything in my power to find a person who had been there before, who had walked the walk, and who had experience to teach and mentor me. I would, in this case see if Bill Gates or Michael Dell or someone within their linear sphere of influence would consider being a mentor to me. Would they do it for free? Doubtful, but perhaps they would have a mentoring program. If they didn't, I would again try to find someone with this knowledge who did.

OK, forget computers and back to making money in real estate investing, something I am good at doing. As I look back on my early days in this business, it took time, dedication, passion, effort, faith, and without a doubt the guidance of mentors and advisors in my circle of influence to help me know what I know and to get to where I am today.

Quite simply, it is this knowledge, relationships, and affiliations that changed my life forever – and that's God's honest truth!

BRIAN'S ULTIMATE RESOURCE

If you like the information that I'm giving you in this book, then it is essential that you take the next step. To test drive me and everything I'm about as a mentor, coach, and advisor to real estate investors all over the country, make sure you take action and get "The Most Incredible Free Real Estate Money Making Gift on the Planet, Guaranteed," a $1,620.94 value which, again, is yours absolutely free, no strings attached. If you say yes (which you should or you're crazy), you will receive a package of money-making goodies that I will deliver to you like a pizza to your door. The total value of this gift will blow your mind! Simply go to www.FreeMakeMoneyGift.com. You'll pay a small shipping and handling fee but, in return, you get $1,620.94 worth of millionaire real estate information. Limited Supply Available.

Naturally, a coach or mentor needs to be qualified to give you the most benefit, so choose carefully. The confidence that a coach or mentor gives you can be tremendous, because as you grow your business, you have a partner of sorts (at least in mind or spirit) who can guide you through your early development. Some seminar programs offer these types of mentors and others can be found through networking locally. I highly recommend this tool and have met many successful investors who benefited from coaching and mentoring, so take my advice to heart. This one piece of advice could potentially shorten your learning curve and enhance your initial chances for success as a real estate investor better than any other training tool available.

BRIAN'S JOURNAL ENTRY

"My First Mentor in the Business"

When my retail coffee shop business failed, I knew that I needed to pick a direction to go from there. My choices were (1) pursue the passion that I had acquired for real estate from my books or (2) go find a nine-to-fiver. Well, since I wasn't married, didn't have children, and didn't have money, I decided that I didn't have much to lose so, you guessed it, I went after my passion for real estate investing.

After doing some networking in my area, it turned out that one of my business relationship friends knew someone who was active in real estate investing. The problem was, he lived 80 miles away. I asked my friend to introduce me to this guy. Little did this investor know at the time that I was a man on a mission and was going to work for him whether he liked it or not.

With time, I professionally pursued the new relationship and became an apprentice, if you will, to this investor. It really was a win-win relationship. I would drive over an hour each way every day to work for this guy and was willing to do whatever it took for him to enlighten me about the business. Overall, it was about a six-month period where I wasn't making a penny, but I was getting an invaluable education about how to make money as a real estate investor.

Eventually, the time came where I was either going to move and work for this guy full-time or stay home and start my own real estate investing business based on the knowledge that I had acquired. At the time, it was the scariest choice I had ever made, but I decided to make a go of it on my own. I was extremely fortunate to have been able to experience the business from someone already in it. This mentor-mentee relationship was invaluable in helping me gain confidence and get started as a real estate investor. I wouldn't wish for it any other way.

BRIAN'S ULTIMATE RESOURCE

Having a mentor was so beneficial to me in my early days that I have made it a personal commitment of mine to reciprocate and give back to other aspiring real estate investors looking to achieve great success in this business.

Do I get paid for sharing my knowledge and wisdom to help other people make their fortunes? Absolutely, and everyone wins in the end. If establishing a mentor/mentee relationship with me is something that you want and are prepared to invest in, then take action right now. <u>Simply send a one-page fax to me at 859-201-1441. Mention in the fax that you read this book and that you would like to be considered for one-on-one coaching.</u> My staff will send you an application for coaching and I will personally decide, based on that application, if you are ready, willing, and able to turn your real estate investing dreams into reality. The number of students I coach at any one time is capped and applications are considered on a first-come-first-serve basis, so don't delay if this is your goal.

EXPERIENCE, AKA THE SCHOOL OF HARD KNOCKS

Some investors adamantly argue that this form of education is second to none, but I don't think of it as a prerequisite to quickly becoming an ultimate real estate investor. I'll be the first to admit that experience is a necessary part of an investor's so-called curriculum. After all, what good is the rest of an educational package if it is not put to use in the real world? Experience-based education is certainly valuable in its own right and can be a mixture of both good and bad experiences, such as:

- Facing litigation

- Having to go to court to evict a tenant

- Having tenants trash a property before they move out

- Losing an escrow deposit

- Taking a loss on a property that ended up being a money pit

There are other examples but this gives you the idea. Experience can make us wise to what happens down the road and, in the absence of some background education, can also be quite painful and expensive. Experience can and should be considered a beneficial supplement to other forms of training (the types of training that can help you avoid certain key pitfalls in the first place). Using a well-rounded mix of education is perhaps the most valuable thing you can do and can perhaps keep you from blindly accepting what comes your way as just a part of the learning process.

Experience is something that all investors gain over time, and I've always found it helpful whenever possible to benefit from the experiences of others before embarking on something new myself. Teachers who are willing to share both their knowledge and their past experiences (the good and the bad) are abundant in the world of real estate; why not take advantage of this before having to experience all the ups and downs yourself, as if you were the first person who ever tried? Take my word for it, there is no substitute for experience in this business. You just don't have to experience all the possible mistakes and poor decisions yourself to learn from these mistakes. We've all made mistakes, and we've all made bad decisions – anyone who has been in this business for a while, as I have, can certainly attest to that. Learn from this, learn from the experiences of others, and your own educational journey will be a smoother path to success in real estate investing.

The bottom line is this: Education is not just a hot topic for the news media and for politicians. It is an essential part of being successful in any kind of business. Just to remind you, you don't need a traditional education (e.g., a business degree, an MBA) to be successful in this business. Numerous studies have shown that traditional education, despite what benefits it offers and value it may have, is anything but a solid indicator of future financial success.

BRIAN'S KEY POINT

You must constantly invest in your education as a real estate investor if you want to achieve great success and longevity.

That said, businesses don't succeed alone on pure drive and determination, although it could be argued that these things are ultimately what helps keep businesses afloat through growing pains and other challenges. In short, your vision and courage are most admirable, but they aren't a substitute for properly educating yourself on the nuances of your business. You still need to be able to understand the numbers, prepare paperwork, evaluate market conditions, interact with people, negotiate effectively, and ultimately determine the profitability of the real estate deals you pursue.

The adage "Do your own homework" has multiple applications in the world of real estate investing. Sure, it can refer to proper evaluation of deals, adequate due diligence, or even timely reliance on your professional team. I will discuss these things more in Chapter 5. In the here and the now, the idea of doing your homework also means getting yourself educated in the business and, if you haven't done enough to this point, there's no better time than now. This book itself is a great resource, and for those of you very new to the business, a nice start. Now, make a commitment to your education and treat this as part of the process just like you would any other aspect of your business. Do so, and success will soon be at your doorstep.

CHAPTER 4

The Attitude of an Ultimate Real Estate Investor

Question: How important is attitude in the world of real estate investing? Answer: Extremely important, so important, in fact, that it can make a huge difference in the overall profitability of your organization. It is essential. This chapter will explore some of the basic components of a successful attitude and how each of these components contributes to your success.

The typical reference to attitude that you will hear is heavily laden with emphasis on always being positive. "Stay positive," or "Be positive," are the two mottos of this approach, and I can't say that I disagree with this at all. I just happen to think there's a little more to it than that. A good attitude has two critical components: What you feel inside and what you convey to the outside world. A good attitude also has more to it than just positive spin. Real components of a positive attitude include:

The Attitude of an Ultimate Real Estate Investor

(Mind Map)

Note that nowhere in the above mind map did you see "raw exuberance" or any reference to the classic smile-and-nod approach to pleasing clients or, in some cases, people very close to us. In short, a good attitude is not about exuding energy or being constantly agreeable. There's just an apparent superficiality to that approach that many clients can see right through. The ultimate investor's approach to a good attitude relies upon the items I listed for you and each of them warrants its own discussion.

FRIENDLINESS

This first component of a good attitude is also perhaps one of the most obvious. Naturally, an investor who comes across as being a bit of a jerk (unfortunately I've met some like this) is not going to be seen as favorably, but those who fit this category probably have their reasons. For example, the jerk might say, "Hey, this is a business, and I just treat it and everyone I'm around as a business." Sure, treating a business like a business is important, but I think a comment like that is just a euphemism for, "I'm a jerk, deal with it." The bottom line is that some people just aren't nice and probably never will be.

You can look at this and shake your head or you can look at it as a golden opportunity. The jerks of the world are going to bring their bad attitudes to the clients and colleagues they meet and that will only make those of us who are friendly look that much better. Just being professional, cordial, polite, and courteous are elements of the friendly investor's approach. The integrity comes not from investment expertise in this case but from just being a decent human being. The value of that alone should never be underestimated. You are in a people business and being likable can go a long way toward your ultimate success.

EMPATHY

Empathy is simply defined as the ability to understand the situation or needs of another person. It is sometimes confused with the similar term, sympathy, but there is a significant difference between the two. Sympathy is to actually feel bad for someone and, in doing so, absorb the emotional impact of someone's situation. Empathy is no less sensitive, but involves less emotion, making empathy a more objective response, which is necessary for us as real estate investors.

The way that empathy manifests itself is simply to be interested in someone's situation, ask questions, and legitimately want to understand what is going on. When you can convey this to your clients, they will respond with a tremendous amount of respect because you actually are interested in what is going on in their lives. Empathy is not just asking questions, though. It is a part of your attitude and will show in both the tonality of how you speak and body language, so your empathy must be sincere in order for it to show to a client.

In the world of real estate investing, it is common to work with clients who are in distressed situations. Empathy is an extremely valuable tool to have in your attitude arsenal, because clients want to be understood more than they want someone just to feel bad for them. Your empathetic attitude keeps a level of business professionalism around your approach, but also shows that you care, which can be a very potent and effective combination.

CONFIDENCE

What exactly is confidence? This state of mind is often misrepresented, and I think unfairly so. Oftentimes, the confident individual who gets a bad rap is seen as arrogant or, in the case of more laid-back demeanors, smug. Is this fair? In many cases, no, but that is how it is, and I would like to offer my opinion here on how to convey confidence without overdoing it.

To best illustrate this, let me offer my definitions for arrogance. Smugness, or at least the perception of it, is just quiet arrogance, so the same definition will apply to both words. Arrogance is a display of confidence that (1) cannot be backed up by real knowledge or experience, (2) is used to demean or patronize another, or (3) both. Arrogance is of course a little more flamboyant and is more noticeable, but smugness can be equally detrimental. Many people who themselves are not confident will see any display of confidence, quiet or exuberant, as smugness or arrogance, even if the label is unwarranted. As you develop more confidence in your business, you must work to make it an effective part of your attitude but also be aware that it can be seen the wrong way. Confidence mixed with the right infusion of humility and simple expression of knowledge may well serve you in avoiding being unfairly tagged as arrogant or smug.

The bottom line here is that confidence can be effectively demonstrated through having good knowledge in a particular area without coming across as a know-it-all. In short, when you educate yourself as an investor, that knowledge will show up at some point in the form of confidence. That first meeting you have with a client when you feel sure of yourself and are able to convey that to the client can be a breakthrough confidence builder. When you can consistently convey knowledge-based confidence, the impact on your local reputation will be significant and can mean great things for your business.

FLEXIBILITY

A significant and important part of an investor's attitude has to include flexibility, which allows the investor to remain adaptive in a variety of situations. Flexibility is generally an admired trait and, perhaps better stated, a lack of flexibility is often a negative. Flexibility is not just having an open schedule for appointments. It is an underlying attitude of open-mindedness that naturally welcomes a variety of scenarios and potential outcomes.

How do you rate yourself on a flexibility scale of 1 to 10? It's OK if you are low or in the middle. The important thing is to be honest with yourself. Many strong personalities may have a "my way or the highway" approach to life and to business and, if this sounds like you, then flexibility is something you likely need to work on.

Fundamentally, flexibility is about being open-minded and envisioning various outcomes for each deal you do. It means you have a general flow of events in mind, but that you are also open to suggestions and some minor deviation from the plotted course. This is a healthy attitude, because few deals go exactly according to plan. Be flexible, and you'll be both more successful and more influential on your clients.

HUMILITY

Humility, as a component of attitude, is a nice counterbalance to confidence. Humility has been an admired trait in people for a long time, and I think, in moderation, it has its place. What I mean by this is that too often investors can overdo the humility and, in doing so, be seen as either soft or weak. This can be a disadvantage when working with other investors or more assertive clients.

The proper dose of humility can actually work to your benefit. Humility is essentially an expression of "Hey, I'm not that different from you," or "I'm no better than you," or "I made a mistake, and I'm sorry," and can be an indirect way to establish an initial rapport with a client. It effectively offsets confidence by adding a certain human side to a display of confidence and makes the client less prone to see your confidence as arrogance.

From a basic attitude standpoint, I think it is effective to truly think of yourself as being an equal of most people you encounter. If you truly believe you are better than someone else, then maybe you are arrogant and should do the best you can with that. Too much humility can make you prone to think you aren't worthy of the success that you do deserve and can foster self-sabotaging behavior. (I believe everyone deserves to be successful, but you have to believe that yourself first in order for it to happen.) As is usually the case, a good attitude is somewhat about the right balance of confidence and humility, which can take you a long way.

BRIAN'S JOURNAL ENTRY

"Example of When I Had to Admit to a Client I Made a Mistake."

There is one situation in particular that comes to mind when I think about when I had to display humility in my business. Basically, I had to swallow my pride, take off my red cape, and humbly try to undo with one of my sellers something that I said I would.

Ironically, this situation involves the same property that I bought subject-to, and with the mold problem and the tenant problem, which I discussed in one of my earlier stories. As a result of all the headaches that I encountered with this property, I ended up making a personal decision to approach the original sellers about a year after I had the property and tell them that I was throwing in the towel and wanted to give the property back to them. That's right, I bought the property subject-to, fixed up the interiors a bit, handled some tenant problems, paid for the mold remediation, and made the payments on their loan as agreed until one day when I simply said, "Enough is enough on this one." I decided to cut my losses and run for peace of mind.

I picked up the phone, called the original sellers, and simply told the truth. I didn't make excuses, but rather took it on the chin, handled the closing costs transferring the property back to them, and apologized for my inability to do what I set out to do on this property. Were they somewhat disappointed by the situation? Sure, but they seemed to understand my position, and I felt as though they could relate with my honesty and humility. In the end we respectfully parted ways.

COMMITMENT TO A FAVORABLE OUTCOME

Underlying the repertoire of every successful real estate investor I've met is a dedicated commitment to a mutually beneficial outcome for every deal they complete. While I'll talk a little more about how this fits in with the skill of negotiation in the next chapter, I think the spirit behind this commitment is a critical part of a good investor attitude. After all, if you are in this business just for the money and do not care what outcome is achieved for your clients, sooner or later that approach will catch up with you. That is just my opinion, and I have seen that greed can go so far but does have a tangible end of the road. I'd love to see you take a more favorable path.

BRIAN'S KEY POINT

A commitment to a favorable outcome is also referred to as a win-win situation.

A commitment to a favorable outcome is more than just a negotiation strategy. It becomes an underlying part of your attitude and could even be more effectively described as a philosophy of sorts for your business. When a real estate investment business has such a philosophy, it carries over to most aspects of how you communicate. The commitment to that ideal outcome will appear in your marketing message, it will be reflected in how you talk to clients and will be more apparent than you think.

Before you know it, this type of philosophical commitment will actually start resulting in more deals. Why? Because this component of your attitude will have permeated every part of your business. You will be seen as more sincere, because people will enjoy talking to you and will be more responsive to your business proposals. I've seen this attitude-based evolution in many an investor, always a fun thing to watch unfold. It can happen for you too, so make the commitment to yourself and to how you will do business; then, it will just be a matter of time.

THERE IS NO SECOND PLACE

There are few things that are more important in business than this subject: having the right mindset and playing the game of business as if there is no second place. Take a moment and say this phrase out loud, "There is no second place. There is no second place. There is no second place."

It is a powerful and gutsy phrase that few business people live by. Are you one of these people?

Let's dissect a few things to see why this phrase is so important. Having the right mindset in business is vitally important to the success and longevity of your business. If you convince yourself and truly believe that there is no second place, your actions and your subconscious mind will feed off of this mindset and in turn allow you to maximize your full potential and achieve your goals.

If you play the game of business and think to yourself that you may not win or succeed but that you'll give it a try anyway, then I can virtually guarantee that you will fall short. The reason the ultra-successful business people are where they are is they have an internal sense and belief about themselves and their ability unlike other people. Does this mean that they always win, succeed at everything they do, or have all the answers before they begin? No, but it does mean that they approach everything they do with a deep internal belief in themselves and their businesses that they will succeed and win the game. Not for one second do they believe that they'll come in second.

Why would anyone play a game with the intention to come in second? They don't. You need to run your business with everything you have and do everything you can to succeed and come in first place. Accept nothing else. And if things go wrong (and they will), simply accept it, learn from it, and keep reaching for the finish line.

But here is the tricky part that may be difficult for you to understand right now. You will never reach the finish line – because there isn't one.

THERE IS NO FINISH LINE

Say what? That's right, there is no finish line. Sounds weird, I know, but let me explain. The majority of entrepreneurs go through life reaching for their goals and doing everything they can to reach the finish line. This is all good and well, but after they reach the finish line they go flat because they achieved what they set out to achieve. The thing is, once you get to the finish line, you find out that it is great for a short period of time but eventually all the hype that you created in your mind isn't so great anymore.

Another way to think about it is like this. Many people go through the ride of life waiting to reach the glorious station at the end of the ride. However, you eventually discover that there is no station but only the ride. So the key is to enjoy the ride along the way, because there is no finish line and there is no station.

So how do you approach business and life as if there is no station and no finish line? I'm glad you asked, and here's how. You need to approach your business with two mindsets: (1) A goal mindset and (2) a growth mindset. With a goal mindset, you are setting goals regularly and working hard to achieve your goals. With a growth mindset, you are aware of the fact that you are setting goals but, even more important than setting out to achieve your goals, you are making sure that you are constantly growing as an entrepreneur. By that I mean you need to constantly challenge yourself and grow your business and learn new things. If it ever feels like your business is smooth sailing and on the easy track, then let me predict that you are about to go flat and hit a wall. I believe that your business needs to be constantly moving uphill with new challenges to allow you to grow and change effectively.

You see, by having a growth mindset as well as a goal mindset you begin to realize that there is no finish line and no station at the end of the ride but only the ride itself. Once you fully understand this concept, you'll be able to better appreciate the challenges in life and business and be more successful as a result.

It is natural that the formation of a good attitude may be something that you need to work on a little bit. I like to believe that many of us are naturally positive, but as you've seen, there's more to a good real estate investor's attitude than just that. It is what goes into a good attitude that will also contribute the most to your success and growth. Why do these things need to be built or worked on?

Well, the basic components of who you are as a person will still shine through in your attitude as a real estate investor. If you are naturally friendly, this will reflect in your attitude. The components like empathy, confidence, and commitment to a favorable outcome may take a little time to develop as you get comfortable in your business and learn more about how things work. For example, it's real easy for someone to say, "Just be confident," but if you are just learning the business, this may be easier said than done. The confidence will come as you build your experiences and absorb more education.

The bottom line is this. Who you are shapes your overall attitude. What you learn and add to your vault of experiences will mold and refine your attitude and your business.

CHAPTER 5

The Skill Sets of an Ultimate Real Estate Investor

Any profession has its basic skill set. Mechanics need to know their way around cars, know how to identify problems, and know how to use tools to remedy those problems. Artists need to not only have a vision but also the basic artistic skills to bring their ideas to life. Professional athletes need to be able to perform at a high level with both athleticism and the skills for the specific sport. As a professional real estate investor, you will need to demonstrate your particular skill set in order to be at the top of your game and thus be seen as reliable by your clients, team, and peers.

It's no surprise that certain skills will benefit you as an investor. It does beg the question, "What are the skills necessary to be a successful real estate investor?" You may have your own ideas on this, and I have mine as well. Some of what I present in this chapter will seem logical and some of it might surprise you. The idea here is to confirm some things you may already be aware of as well as enlighten you to additional skills to help you succeed.

For starters, this list is what I perceive to be the most common sets of skills a real estate investor needs in order to be super successful and even survive in this business. Then, I will elaborate on each so you see exactly where I'm coming from and why I believe these skills are so important. To attempt this business without a firm grasp and understanding of each skill is like jumping out of a plane without a parachute, not a good idea.

The Skill Sets of an Ultimate Real Estate Investor
(Mind Map)

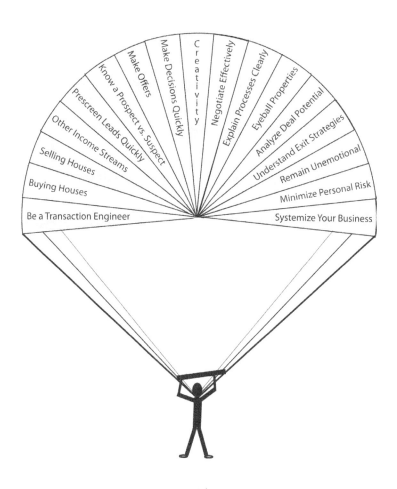

Before I get into the details of these specific skills, I want to point out (as you may have already noticed from the image above) that I did not include things like detailed market knowledge or being handy as essential investor skills. Many investors falsely presume they need to have such skills to be successful in this business, but I just don't agree with that. Those are useful skills but can be delegated to your professional team and thus not critical for your success. With that said, let's look a little closer at the skills I do see as more important.

BE A TRANSACTION ENGINEER

Let me quote the great John D. Rockefeller, who said, "I have ways of making money that you'll never know." Wow, what a powerful and possibly arrogant statement – I love it! It is the perfect opening to what the real point of being an ultimate real estate investor is all about: Making as much money in as many ways as possible!

Right? That's the main reason why you are reading this book and taking advice from me, because I've told you that I can help you make big money as a real estate investor. Well, you are exactly right, I can help you make big money as a real estate investor, and I'm going to give you a no-fluff, "here's what you need to become" glimpse into what it will take if you really, truly, passionately want to be a millionaire real estate investor.

Let's for a moment dissect Rockefeller's quote, "I have ways of making money that you'll never know."

If I asked you how many ways you knew how to make money with real estate, what would your answer be? One, two, three, four, five, or even 10 or 15 ways? If your answer is one way, then you are in or about to be in a serious world of hurt. Anytime you are relying on only one way of doing things, whether it be the way you buy houses, the way you sell houses, the way you do marketing, the attorney you use, the coach you learn from, or any other one thing, then you are setting yourself up for immediate or future problems.

If you want to be a kick-ass and relentlessly confident real estate investor, then *you need to become a transaction engineer*. So what does that mean, to be a transaction engineer? It means that you can take any seller or buyer, fill out my Ultimate Prescreening Seller (UPS) sheet or my Ultimate Prescreening Buyer (UPB) sheet (these are widely used resources that I provide to all my Ultimate Real Estate Investor members, and I'll share them with you in the next few pages). The more ways that you know how to buy and sell real estate, the more money you'll make, the more confident you'll be, the more control you'll have, the more freedom you'll have, and the more secure your life will be.

So let's go a little deeper into this transaction engineer concept and flush out all the ways that you can make money as a real estate investor. Make note that these are the primary ways to get rich in real estate; however, each bullet below can literally be seen as an individual business model all by itself. In fact, I could create dozens of different buying and selling scenarios with each model. To avoid becoming too confusing, I will keep it simple.

BUYING HOUSES

- Buy for cash at a discount: Your cash and credit, partner's cash and credit, private lender, hard-money lender

- Take over debt: Otherwise referred to as buying "subject-to," subject to any existing mortgages on the property, where the ownership is transferred to you, but the mortgage stays in the sellers' name

- Buy with seller financing: Get ownership of a property and ask the seller to agree to carry back a note and mortgage on the home

- Buy on a short sale: Working with a seller who is behind on mortgage payments and negotiating with the lender in an attempt to create a discounted mortgage payoff

- Buy wholesale from other investors: Your cash and credit, partner's cash and credit, private lender, hard-money lender

- Buy or create real estate paper assets: Oftentimes the paper on the real estate can be more valuable to you as the investor if you know how to control or discount it

- Buy on a lease option: Instead of actually buying a home, you could potentially lease the home from a seller with the right to buy it

- Buy in your self-directed Roth IRA: And get tax-free profits for life!

SELLING HOUSES

- Retail the property: Fixing up a home and selling to an end user or owner occupant buyer who will cash you out

- Wholesale a property: Selling a property that you have under contract to another investor who's intent is to rehab and retail the property

- Assign a contract: Alternative to wholesaling, you can simply assign a contract to purchase to another investor buyer and avoid closing on a property altogether

- Lease option or rent-to-own: Collect a nonrefundable option deposit from a tenant buyer and give him or her the right to buy the home and cash you out at a future date

- Monthly cash flow: Received from the monthly payment from your tenant buyer

- Cash-out money: When and/or if your tenant buyer exercises the option to buy

- Sell with seller financing: Sell to a new buyer while you carry back a note and mortgage on a home, also referred to as selling on a land contract, contract for deed, or all-inclusive trust deed

- Sell doing a round-robin auction: Intent is to market a property very heavily and, in a short period of time, to find quickly a cash-out buyer over the period of one weekend

- Sell your seller carry-back note: If you sell using seller financing, you can sell the note at a discount to a note buyer and get cashed out

OTHER INCOME STREAMS

- Sell leads: Did you know that the buyer and seller leads that you generate with your marketing could be worth something to other people? The key is finding people willing to pay you for your information

- Down payment assistance program: Collect additional down payment money, which is nonrefundable, from you tenant buyers over and above their lease payment each month and apply it to their down payment

- Discount carry-back notes prior to cash outs: If you buy on seller financing, you could always request a discount on the note if you pay off early

- Seller pays you to buy his or her home: Sound crazy, doesn't it? Perhaps, but you'd be surprised, as some sellers are desperate enough to offer to pay you to buy their house

- Find deals and bring to a partner to complete: Perhaps you are timid or unsure how to do some deals, so simply bring them to someone who knows how to do them and ask to do a profit split (I do this frequently with some students, and everyone wins)

If only I could take a computer cable and connect it from my brain to yours and let you download my knowledge about all the variables within each of the bullets above about how to make money in real estate investing. Perhaps one day science will make this possible, but until then lets keep going.

The bottom line is, to be a mega-successful or even a moderately successful real estate investor in today's day and age, you *need* to be a transaction engineer. You need to be able to look at a deal and determine quickly all of the various ways you could potentially make money on this deal. I must, however, back up for just a moment and say that the majority of all the deals you'll come across are going to be no good. Whatever you do, don't try so hard to be a transaction engineer that you attempt to create magic deals out of thin air when, in reality, there was never a deal there to begin with. As much as it is a learned skill to be able to structure your purchases and sales in various ways, it is just as much a learned skill to be able to pass on a deal.

BRIAN'S ULTIMATE RESOURCE

I'll close by adding a little personal spin to Rockefeller's quote for the sake of this book, "I have ways of making money as a real estate investor that you will never know," unless, that is, you are an Ultimate Real Estate Investor. Learn more at

www.UltimateRealEstateInvestors.com.

ABILITY TO PRESCREEN LEADS QUICKLY AND EFFECTIVELY

Prescreening your seller and buyer leads is often a challenge for most new real estate investors, because they don't know what type of information to ask for and why. Good news, I have solved this problem for you. Below are the exact two prescreening sheets that I and all my students use when gathering information from sellers and buyers. After completing the UPS and UPB sheets, you'll have all the information you need to determine whether the lead is a prospect or a suspect.

ULTIMATE PRESCREENING SELLER (UPS) SHEET

Brian Evans': Ultimate Prescreening SELLER (UPS) Sheet

VIP Members may Fax this form to 859-201-1441 a maximum of 5 times per month for Basic Deal Prescreening Advice from Brian Evans. Replies will be within 48 business hours and will be sent by fax or email. Starred areas must be completed or Brian will not reply to the submission. Phone discussion & additional prescreenings are only for Gold, Platinum & Mastermind Members.

★ Name _____
★ Email _____
★ Best Phone Number _____
★ Fax Number _____

GENERAL SELLER INFORMATION

Name (s) _____ Day Phone _____
How Did You Hear About Us? _____ Evening Phone _____
Email _____ Cell Phone _____
Property Address _____
City _____ State _____ Zip _____
Bedrooms _____ Stories / Floors _____
Bathrooms _____ Garage ○ None ○ Yes If Yes, type/style _____
Square Footage _____ Basement ○ Slab ○ Crawl ○ Partial ○ Full ○ Unfinished
Year Built _____ Lot Size/Acres _____ Anyone else on the deed? _____

SITUATION

★ What is your situation / Why are you selling?

What is your timeframe / How soon would you like to move? _____
How long has the property been for sale? _____
Is there anyone living in the house?   ○ Yes- Owner Occupied   ○ Yes- Tenant   ○ No- Unoccupied

ARV (AFTER REPAIRED VALUE)

★ What do you think the house would appraise for if I had it appraised? _____

REPAIRS

What is the current condition of your property?   ○ Excellent   ○ Good   ○ Fair   ○ Poor   ○ Terrible
What kind of repairs/maintenance does the house need?

★ What do you think the repairs will cost?   ○ Less than $5k   ○ $5k-$10k   ○ $10k-$15k   ○ $15k-$20k   ○ $20k+

ASKING PRICE

★ How much are you asking for the house? _____
How did you determine your asking price?   ○ Realtor   ○ Appraisal   ○ Tax Assessment   ○ Best Guess
Is the house currently listed with a Realtor?   ○ Yes   ○ No   If yes, when does listing expire? _____

LOAN INFORMATION

★ Any Mortgages on your property?   ○ Yes   ○ No   Any other liens or judgments? _____

1st Mortgage	2nd Mortgage
★ Balance Owed _____	★ Balance Owed _____
★ Monthly Payment _____	★ Monthly Payment _____
Interest Rate _____	Interest Rate _____
★ Type of Loan ○30 Yr. Conv ○ARM ○FHA ○VA	★ Type of Loan ○30 Yr. Conv ○ARM ○FHA ○VA
★ Payments Current ○ Yes ○ No	★ Payments Current ○ Yes ○ No
★ If No, how far behind? _____	★ If No, how far behind? _____
Taxes & Ins. in the payment? ○ Yes ○ No	Taxes & Ins. in the payment? ○ Yes ○ No

BRIAN'S KEY POINT

If you do nothing else when prescreening sellers, make sure that you determine the (1) ARV, after repaired value, (2) asking price, (3) loan information, (4) repairs needed, and (5) reason for selling.

ULTIMATE PRESCREENING BUYER (UPB) SHEET

Brian Evans': Ultimate Prescreening BUYER (UPB) Sheet

VIP Members may Fax this form to 859-201-1441 a maximum of 5 times per month for Basic Deal Prescreening Advice from Brian Evans. Replies will be within 48 business hours and will be sent by fax or email. Starred areas must be completed or Brian will not reply to the submission. Phone discussion & additional prescreenings are only for Gold, Platinum & Mastermind Members.

★ Name _____
★ Email _____
★ Best Phone Number _____
★ Fax Number _____

GENERAL BUYER INFORMATION

Name (s) _____   Day Phone _____

How Did You Hear About Us? _____   Evening Phone _____

Email _____   Cell Phone _____

Current Address _____

City _____   State _____   Zip _____

Buyer's Property Needs

What Property Are You Interested In? _____

★ How Do You Want to buy?   ○ Lease to Own   ○ Owner Finance   ○ Cash Purchase   ○ Get New Loan

★ What Is The Most You Can Afford to Pay Monthly For Your New Home? _____

★ What Is The Most You Can Afford to Put Down on Your New Home? _____

What Price Range Houses Are You Looking For? _____

★ How Is Your Credit?   ○ Excellent   ○ Good   ○ Bad   ○ OK   ○ Ugly

Have You Ever Filed Bankruptcy? _____

Have You Ever Been Foreclosed On? _____

Any Car Repossessions? _____

What If Anything Would a Lender Not Like about Your Credit Report? _____

Do You Have Any Idea What Your Credit Score Is? _____

How Soon Are You Looking To Purchase Your Next Home? _____

What Area Do You Want To Live In? _____

How Many Bedrooms Do You Need? _____

How Many Bathrooms Do You Need? _____

How Many Square Feet Do You Need? _____

Do You Have Any Other Special Requirements For Your Next Home? _____

BRIAN'S KEY POINT

If you do nothing else when prescreening buyers, make sure that you determine (1) what is the most they can put for the down payment, (2) what is the most they can afford to pay monthly, and (3) is their credit good, bad, or ugly?

KNOWING THE DIFFERENCE BETWEEN A PROSPECT AND A SUSPECT

You will come across lots of sellers who will want to sell you their house, when in reality the only person who should buy their house is someone who wants to pay full price and live in it.

The following criteria are what you should be on the lookout for when determining a prospect vs. a suspect.

A prospect is:

- Someone who expresses a high level of motivation to sell his or her house

- Someone who is flexible in how he or she will sell their house to you

- Someone whose asking price is at least $20,000 and/ or 20%-30% less than what the house is worth in good condition

- Someone who is behind in mortgage payments or about to be

- Someone who has no debt on the property and is willing to owner-finance to you

A suspect is:

- Someone who wants to sell his or her house rather than needs to sell the house

- Someone who won't share mortgage information with you

- Someone who won't return phones calls

- Someone who is uncooperative and over-demanding

- Someone who makes you feel uncomfortable when working with him or her

BRIAN'S KEY POINT

Always remember, you are an investor and the only way you buy houses is if you can enter the deal with little or no money down and find a way to make a substantial profit with minimal risk. Otherwise you have no reason to get involved in the deal.

ABILITY TO MAKE OFFERS

Getting your phone to ring and collecting information from sellers using the UPS sheet are two vital steps to success in this business. Unfortunately, it's the inability to make offers that keeps most novice investors from making money. I've seen many people enter this business with great intentions, send out a bunch of letters to a specific list, get prescreened calls from prospects through their live operator script, yet never call these sellers back because they are too afraid of the human interaction. This may sound crazy to some of you, but others of you can probably relate.

I am sorry to be the one to burst your preconceived bubble, but in order to make millions, you have to be able to interact with sellers every day and make lots of offers on properties. Just know that most of the offers you make will not get accepted. Think of it as a numbers game, so the more offers you make, the more deals you do; the fewer offers you make, the fewer deals you do. It is as simple as that.

When making offers, don't complicate the situation. Just have a normal, honest conversation with the person on the other end of the phone. Remember, that person called you with a house for sale. Just be sure that you have given some thought to your potential offers ahead of time. Also, multiple offers that you can present to sellers on ways you may be able to buy their houses will always be better than just one.

ABILITY TO MAKE DECISIONS QUICKLY

Quick decision-making and the ability to take action is one of the hallmark skills of a successful real estate investor. Note that I am not suggesting in any way that decisions be rash or careless. What I'm referring to instead is the efficiency and timeliness in which decisions get made. The more knowledgeable you are, coupled with ever-increasing levels of experience, the easier it will become to make decisions quickly. There are several reasons why this is such a valuable skill.

First, quick decision-making puts you in line to capitalize on those great deals that you are exposed to in the course of running your business. Slow decisions and too much analysis lead to great deals being lost and I don't want to see this happen to you. Too many real estate investors, especially beginners, get what is called "paralysis of analysis." They get stuck analyzing the numbers over and over, the neighborhood, the situation, etc., only to find out that they just analyzed themselves right out of the deal before they even made an offer, yet alone gotten a property under contract. This is not the way ultimate investors do business. If this sounds like you, then break this habit immediately. Get a property under contract and then do your due diligence, not the other way around.

After you have done all your due diligence, ask yourself, "What's the worst that can happen?" If you can prevent the worst from happening before you close on a property, then do it. If you can't, but still want to proceed, just make sure that your decision won't keep you awake at night. If it won't, then you should probably do the deal. If it will, then you should probably walk away. Keep in mind that this discussion is about being efficient with your decisions. This might only happen a couple of times before you really start seeing the value of this skill. Remember, I am primarily talking about making offers here. You can make a quick decision and still have time for due diligence, so don't think of this as opening you up to greater risk, because that isn't the case.

You see, creating a successful business is all about making difficult decisions, taking educated risks, facing your fears, taking action, overcoming adversity, and never giving up. As the business owner, you and only you are responsible for what happens in your life and the success that you achieve or don't achieve. Knowing this, the next time you are faced with a difficult decision, ask yourself, "What's the worst that could happen?"

It is very easy to get overwhelmed by the fear and anxiety that running and growing a business brings your way. Trust me, I, too, am trying to grow my business every day, just like you. These feelings are very familiar to me, but I deal with them by asking myself that same question.

So, before you throw in the towel or decide against taking action with a business or investment decision, make sure that you ask yourself, "What's the worst that could happen?" I think you will begin to find that your decisions aren't as difficult to make after you implement this simple tactic.

Second, quick decisions give you valuable experience in thinking on the fly and getting into the habit of acting and responding as if your income depended on it. This will not only benefit your business but also give you valuable confidence that you can keep up with the pros out there and that you are more than just a newbie. Most people get a feeling about something, analyze this feeling, and then act. I've trained my mind to do the opposite. I prefer to make a decision and then deal with the feelings and repercussions after the fact. Have I made mistakes based on this method of thinking? Sure. However, my successes have always greatly outweighed my mistakes, and therefore I have no doubt that this learned skill has greatly attributed to the achievements of my business.

Lastly, one of the greatest benefits of quick decision-making is the boost it will give to your authority. Clients and peers alike will respect your ability to think and act quickly, establishing you as a force to be reckoned with.

BRIAN'S JOURNAL ENTRY

"A Motto That I Try to Live By"

A motto that I try to live by, which may or may not be right for the average entrepreneur but is right for me, is, "Act and then feel." What I mean by this is that I try to make an educated decision on something and then deal with the feelings or repercussions of my actions after the fact. Please note that this motto has nothing to do with the saying, "Fire, then aim." I'm not saying that. I know that some business people preach the fire-then-aim attitude, but not me. I think it is very important to aim before you fire, no matter what you are doing.

The difference between my motto and the other is this: A lot of people aim and think and analyze a decision for way too long and eventually analyze themselves right out of any action at all. Contrary to this, I believe that speed, action, and results go hand in hand. At some point, you have to simply decide to take action or not. If I don't have all, but enough of the facts that I feel I can make an educated decision and live with the consequences, then I'll try to quickly implement the action before I have a chance to let my fears and anxieties get in the way of my decision. This might also be referred to as acting on gut instinct. Everyone has this gut instinct, but it is up to you to hone in and develop it to help you make decisions quickly and effectively.

CREATIVITY

Creativity in real estate is one of those unsung skills that can easily and effectively set you apart from your competition. Note that I am not referring to creativity in the artistic or left-brained vs. right-brained sense. Creativity in real estate means being willing, able, and committed to outside-the-box thinking and bringing that philosophy to every aspect of your business. There are several primary areas of your business where this will benefit you.

First, you have marketing. Marketing is one of the easiest arenas in which you can express yourself creatively, and it doesn't just mean having the most unique appearance to your marketing message or media. It just means having a nice diversified approach to marketing your business and, by doing so, going the extra mile that your competition will not. Second, you have your actual approach to working with clients. Creativity here may mean nothing more than just being a good person and presenting yourself in a way your clients will not be accustomed to. Anything that sets you apart from other investors can be a form of creative expression, and such things will benefit you.

You want to have command of the fundamentals of real estate investing so you objectively are seen as competent. Beyond the basics, a creative or otherwise unique approach to your business will demonstrate that you aren't afraid to march to the beat of your own drum and be comfortable doing so. Peers and clients alike will respect what makes you unique.

ABILITY TO NEGOTIATE EFFECTIVELY

Negotiation is another fundamental skill that all ultimate real estate investors possess and is probably one of my personal skills that has made me most successful, setting me apart from any other real estate investor our there. Plus, it's fun to negotiate. So why is it so important? Negotiation is involved in everything you do, from establishing a professional team, interacting with clients, and getting your deals tied up and completed, and is a vital component to this business and, whether you educate yourself or get trained or simply learn by getting out there and working deals, this is definitely something you need to master.

MY PERSONAL 12 COMMANDMENTS TO NEGOTIATION SUCCESS

1. Educate yourself as to what all parties are trying to achieve

2. Ask good questions

3. Listen to what the other party has to say

4. Understand the needs of the other party

5. Have the courage to ask for what you want

6. Don't necessarily accept no for an answer

7. Be prepared to deal with opposition or objections to what you present

8. Learn to ask the same thing in different ways, multiple times

9. Be able to justify your requests with confidence

10. Don't make decisions based on desperation, impatience, or emotion

11. Be prepared to give if you receive and vice versa

12. Have the wisdom to know when to walk away

Focusing on these key areas does not have to be a monumental task. Just be committed to the fundamentals outlined above and remember that most anything is negotiable. Never just take things for granted and presume you have no opportunity to negotiate, because few things are truly like that, in life or in business. A mentor of mine said it best, "What comes out of your mouth goes into your bank account." The worst thing that people can say to a request you make is no and if that happens simply ask for something else or ask in a different way.

BRIAN'S KEY POINT

If you take away anything from this section on negotiation, let it be this: You will never get what you don't ask for.

Your commitment to being a good negotiator will be apparent to your clients and to your peers. Your goal is not necessarily to be seen as shrewd, but rather as someone who is always open to discussion and willing to find the ideal outcome that benefits everyone involved. This commitment should become a part of your business philosophy.

ABILITY TO EXPLAIN COMPLEX PROCESSES CLEARLY

As a real estate investor, it is imperative that you recognize and respect that your knowledge of the business makes you fairly unique. Most of your clients and many of your peers will not have the same knowledge as you, and you need to be ready to explain things properly in so-called layperson's terms or third-grade English so that you communicate effectively with everyone. Never assume, for example, that a client understands the foreclosure process in your area or that another investor speaks the language of real estate investing as you do. This approach will generally serve you well.

FOUR TIPS TO HELP YOU COMMUNICATE MORE CLEARLY

1. Ask probing questions that presume the client or peer knows what you are talking about; this way you'll avoid unnecessarily patronizing them if they are more knowledgeable

2. Welcome feedback, so if a client or peer is not up to speed with what you are talking about, they'll feel comfortable asking you questions

3. Use analogies to explain concepts to draw parallels between real estate and things a client may be more familiar with

4. Avoid terms that might confuse or scare away your client. For example, instead of saying contract or purchase and sales agreement say, "This is the piece of paper that says you are selling the home and I am buying it." Instead of saying this is the deed, say, "This is the piece of paper that transfers ownership in the property from you to me." Instead of asking if a seller will-owner finance, ask "Will you allow me to make payments to you for the house?"

By following these tips, you'll be more effective as a communicator. When you can effectively communicate, you will be seen as more convincing, because part of effective communication is making sure the other party knows and understands what you are talking about.

ABILITY TO EYEBALL PROPERTIES

What I call "eyeballing properties" is something of a two-headed skill set for the real estate investor. Part one of the skill is to be able to see potential where others may not. For example, have you ever driven past a property and found yourself making a judgment about whether it was occupied or had income potential? This premature judgment of a property's potential has likely cost hundreds of investors the chance to secure a great deal, usually without the investor ever realizing it. Look at everything as having potential. This may seem pretty basic, but it is a skill because most investors have to train themselves to look at properties liberally.

Part two of this skill set is to be able to quickly evaluate the condition of a particular property. Many new investors will downplay their ability to assess a property's flaws (and necessary improvements), but this is not as hard as you might think. First, you should have a contractor on your team who can back you up during your due diligence period. Second, it's not hard to take a trip to the hardware store and price different things that you may need to do to renovate properties. Between these two things, you can quickly develop the skill to estimate repairs (even if it's only a rough estimate) and this skill will give you tremendous confidence. Ultimately, your initial estimated repairs on a property should quickly be $5k, $10k, $15k, $20k, or

$25k. Anything over $25k is a pretty serious rehab which may require additional attention and expertise.

ABILITY TO ANALYZE DEAL POTENTIAL

Real estate is a people business, but will ultimately always come down to the numbers. For the new investor – and especially those who don't think much of their math skills – this can be a daunting proposition. I remember thinking this way a long time ago, and for every investor, overcoming this obstacle is both essential and unique in how you get the job done. For some, simple repetition and doing numbers time and time again helps the process sink in. For others, the use of simple formulas for different situations is a path to success in number-crunching. However you see this part of the business playing out for you, make the commitment to get comfortable with running numbers because your business depends on it.

All that said, I have a few tips and suggestions that I think will help you become more comfortable with this part of the business. First, don't overcomplicate it. Too many investors crunch numbers with the perpetual fear that they are missing something important. Remember my mention of the "paralysis of analysis"? If this is holding you back, estimate costs conservatively and evaluate deals under worst-case scenario conditions. That way you'll feel more comfortable with what you come up with, and you'll be able to proceed more confidently. Another way to feel more confident with number-crunching is to realize that you need to run only a crude set of numbers before making offers on properties. You have plenty of due diligence time after a contract is signed to check your calculations and make adjustments as necessary, so don't feel like you have to be right on the mark from day one.

BRIAN'S JOURNAL ENTRY

"How I Use the MAO Formula"

The primary formula that I use in my business when pursuing the purchase of most properties is the MAO Formula: ARV x 70% - repairs = MAO. This formula for "maximum allowable offer" is somewhat standard throughout the real estate investing marketplace.

Explanation: ARV is "after repaired value," basically what a property is worth fixed up in excellent condition and is multiplied by 70% (this number is a combination of the profit you want to make on a deal, holding costs, and other miscellaneous costs), and then subtracted by the repairs that the property will need to be fixed up to excellent condition, which equals your MAO (the maximum amount that you may be willing to pay for a property in order to make the deal profitable enough for you to pursue).

Therefore, if I was pursuing a property where the seller is asking $82,000, and after some due diligence I determined that the ARV on this property is $120,000 but needs $10,000 in repairs, my formula would look like:

$120,000 AVR x 70% - $10,000 repairs = $74,000 MAO

Knowing this, my goal would be to try to buy the property at or below the MAO (preferably below). I always stick to this formula any time I am making cash-out offers to the seller where I am planning to purchase a property with the only exit strategy being to fix and resell it at its highest value or to wholesale the property for a quick $5,000-$20,000 to another investor who will rehab *the home with his or her money. Based on the above example, if retailing or wholesaling is my exit strategy, then I would need to negotiate with the seller to get a lower purchase price than the $82k they are asking.*

They only time that it would be OK for me to deviate from this formula is when I am purchasing on terms (seller-financing or subject-to). If the seller doesn't need to be cashed out and will carry back a note on the property or allow me to take over the payments, then I may deviate from the formula; however, I still use the formula as a reference point on all my deals.

Obtaining a strong grasp of this MAO formula is very important, because it helps you to prescreen deals quickly, allowing you to focus only on the low-hanging fruit. For example, if you went to pick an apple to eat from a tree, you wouldn't climb the tree and pick the apple at the top. Rather, you would pick the apple closest to your reach. Same thing holds true for real estate deals. I would much rather you weed through a hundred non-deals to find the good deal rather than trying to stretch a non-deal into a deal. Being willing to walk away is just as important as being able to take action. Lastly, always set yourself up to make good money with bad numbers. Murphy lives everywhere, so if something bad can happen, it very likely will happen. This is not a big deal, just prepare for it in the beginning.

If you attempt a deal where the numbers must align perfectly, then this is a deal you should walk away from. Always have a comfortable cushion so that you can make good money with bad numbers. Don't stress, my friend; you'll develop these skills as you continue to learn and grow. Just remember that your ability to do this will produce more profitability for your operation.

ABILITY TO UNDERSTAND EXIT STRATEGIES

There's an old adage that you make your money when you purchase real estate, but when do you actually get paid on most transactions? Sure, it's when you sell, and that points to mastery of exit strategies as a fundamental skill for real estate investors.

BRIAN'S KEY POINT

There are lots of ways to buy, lots of ways to sell. Always remember that the better you get at buying, the easier it is to sell — and make your money.

As previously discussed in the transaction engineer section, there are various exit strategies for you to choose, and all depend on the method you used to purchase a property. I often teach that the best way to determine the quality of a deal is to look at how many different exit strategies will work. The more that work, the better the deal.

Your income is tied to how well you structure your method of purchase on a home, thereby setting up your possible exit strategies. Your profits literally depend on this learned skill, and the best advice I can give you is to make your decisions expeditiously and with absolute conviction. A decision made quickly is not necessarily done in haste; rather, it is efficient and shows the confidence you have in your own decision-making power.

Having conviction in your decisions builds confidence. Sure, you may look back later and realize that an alternate exit might have been better for a particular deal, but the one you did choose made money for you, right? OK then, stick by what you decided, and add the results to your mental database so you can consider different options the next time around. This approach will give you confidence and impress your peers and clients.

ABILITY TO REMAIN UNEMOTIONAL ABOUT BUSINESS

Another old adage, "It's just business," is the foundation for this valuable investor skill. In short, you must be able to separate business from your emotions to operate at peak efficiency.

There are several reasons that emotion can creep into the business of real estate investing, such as:

- Real estate is a people business, and people have emotions

- People often have emotional ties to their homes

- Transactions involve money, and people tend to get funny about money

- Some deals involve stressful or emotionally charged situations in a client's life

BRIAN'S JOURNAL ENTRY

"One of My First Meetings With a Seller"

During my early days, I recall meeting with a seller whose house I was interested in buying. I was still very green and wet behind the ears.

During my meeting with the seller, I was offered coffee and gladly accepted. We started talking and getting to know each other. At the time I thought I was building rapport. About an hour and a half later, I ended up leaving without an agreement to buy the house, scratching my head all the way home wondering what went wrong.

I quickly realized that the last thing you ever want to do when meeting with a seller is think you have to become friends. The truth is, people in these situations aren't looking for a new friend. They are only looking for someone who they believe can solve their problem. This is a very important lesson if you want to be an ultimate real estate investor. Don't accept invitations for food or drink, don't have long story times with people, don't become new friends.

Go there as a business professional who is cognizant of the time, ask specific questions, only get the information that you need, and then get out. They will respect you and look up to you more if you maintain your professional distance.

Recognition of where emotion can come from is one thing. It is another to rise above it and choose not to let your emotions get in the way of good business. I know, easier said than done. This is likely a skill that many investors will need more work to develop than other skills, but it is worth the effort. You don't have to be so unemotional that people see you as a lifeless drone, and don't confuse lack of emotion with lack of personality. Your personality should be on full display, but the onus is on you to not let your emotions dictate your decisions.

BRIAN'S KEY POINT

If you remember anything from this skill, remember this: Fall in love with the numbers, not with the house.

Keeping your emotions out of the picture is more in reference to not letting a client's emotional state affect how you do business or what proposal you make. It means not taking business issues personally. It means stepping back if you feel yourself getting emotionally wrapped up in a business setting and regrouping. These kinds of things will help you avoid bad situations and will also add an air of professionalism to how you conduct yourself.

ABILITY TO MINIMIZE PERSONAL RISK

Similar to keeping one's emotions out of the equation, minimizing personal risk also has a lot to do with how you interact with a particular client. Sure, there is the asset protection component of minimizing personal risk, but that is the subject of a later chapter. What I'm referring to here is the tendency for many new investors to try so hard to accommodate a distressed client that they end up compromising their own business in the process. Examples of how this could happen include:

- Accepting less-than-ideal rents or deposits from tenants or buyers

- Agreeing to a higher purchase price to accommodate a seller's needs

- Agreeing to give a client funds to move or get back on his or her feet

- Agreeing to refinance a property to get a slightly better interest rate

- Agreeing to accept existing tenants from a motivated landlord and having to evict them yourself

- Assuming or personally guaranteeing a debt

I could go on and on and you might ask yourself, "Why would I ever do these things?" The answer is that there are no reasons, and yet it happens with some frequency all the time. How, you ask? It's called emotion, and these things can happen in the so-called heat of battle. When a desperate seller's situation and a strong desire to create a deal come together, sometimes that can lead you to bad decisions that you most definitely want to avoid.

BRIAN'S KEY POINT

My best suggestion is to approach each and every deal you do as if you have zero money or credit and therefore have to structure the deal accordingly to make it work. This forces you to think creatively and, as a result to minimize personal risk. Therefore, always remember that everytime you write a check you are at risk.

Let me repeat myself in case you are not paying attention here, because this is very important to the life, growth, and longevity of your business. Approach every deal as if you have zero money or credit. If you can't make money without money, then you can't make money with money. Even though I gave you this great advice, I know that many of you will use your money and credit anyway.

BRIAN'S ULTIMATE RESOURCE

If you still don't know how to invest in real estate without using your money or credit, you need to go to

www.UltimateRealEstateInvestors.com to discover how.

There's nothing wrong with being compassionate and wanting to help someone. Compassion is exhibited by real estate investors on a regular basis, and most still make good money in the process. It becomes a challenge when your benevolence affects your business decisions. Don't let a client's problems become your problems. Business is business, you didn't put clients in a bad situation, and it isn't up to you to bail them out. There's simply too much at stake to take on the burdens of a client, especially when it affects your business's bottom line.

ABILITY TO SYSTEMIZE YOUR BUSINESS

First I'll talk about why you need to systemize. As you are becoming more and more aware, real estate investing is a real business that needs to be treated like a business. And just like any business that strives to grow and make money, it needs systems in place so it can operate smoothly. Developing and using systems improves your ability to:

- Manage time

- Minimize wasted energy

- Multiply creativity

- Maximize progress

- Enjoy your business

- Think bigger

- Manage cash flow

- Grow your business

- Reduce waste

- Keep people accountable

And the list could go on.

The key thing to remember is this: In order for you to get the most from systemizing, the systems *must* become a lifestyle, not a one-time deal. The truly successful business people understand and implement this. Do you?

Now I'll discuss what you need to systemize in your business. Systemizing can either make or break a business, and if you are getting by in your business right now and don't have solid systems in place, then I would venture to guess that your lack of systems might eventually win the war and put you out of business. That is how serious this topic is.

The most important part of your business that needs to be systemized is the front end, which involves locating and prescreening leads (sellers and buyers). You absolutely *always* need to keep your buying machine running no matter what. You are allowed to turn it down now and again, but never allowed to turn it off.

1. Locating sellers

    a. Acquire the list: Once a week, you or someone who works for you needs to be gathering new prospects for your weekly mailings. For example, in my business we do a lot of direct mail to locate the types of sellers we want to buy from, and drop our letters in the mail every Tuesday.

    b. Market to the list: Once a week, you or someone who works for you needs to be mailing to your collected list of potential sellers automatically.

2. Prescreening sellers

    a. Capture and prescreen the calls from sellers by sending them to your live operator service or to an automatic voice mail set up for them to call. I strongly prefer you to send the calls to a live operator service. Again, the live operator service that I use in my business is PATLive. You can learn more about its services at www.patlive.com/signup/brianevans.

    b. Get in to the habit of calling the new leads back immediately, and call them back in blocks rather than one in the morning and one in the afternoon. Get them all done in one shot every day or every other day.

3. Prescreening buyers

    a. Capture calls from potential buyers by making sure the number they call goes to an automatic mailbox system that gives them information about your buying programs and the houses that you have for sale.

b. Put lock boxes on the houses you have for sale with signs in the yard, and give people the lock box code to view the house without an appointment. You'll be surprised how much easier this is on you and the potential buyer.

c. Give potential buyers instructions when in the house or on your voice mail about what to do when they exit the house and what to do if they like the house.

d. Follow up.

Are these *all* the systems that you need to set up? Absolutely not, but these are the most important ones. The other systems that you need in your business will depend on who you are and how you do business. The bottom line is, set up the front-end systems and the rest will fall into place.

As I wrap up this chapter on investor skill sets, I hope you see a little bit of the philosophy behind how I look at this business. I don't believe you have to do all of this yourself. I don't believe you must have the best market knowledge to be successful. What I do believe is that the most successful investors out there are able to absorb the information presented to them, determine from it what they need to make quick decisions, and rely upon their team and resource network to help confirm the validity of every transaction they pursue.

Beyond the basic elements of making streamlined yet informed decisions, successful real estate investing is about effective communication. How you communicate is the essential merit of your business, the solutions you come up with, and the mutual benefit of the outcomes from your efforts, is absolutely critical to your success. It is natural that you may not feel that you possess all of the skills I've discussed here in this chapter. If so, then they should become a part of your educational process and goals for you to strive to achieve. Each and every one of you has the potential to be a great investor. Sometimes, all it takes is to know where you need to focus your efforts, and I hope this chapter has been helpful in doing just that.

CHAPTER 6

The Passion of an Ultimate Real Estate Investor

What does it mean to be passionate? Passion has obvious connotations in the world of romance, but also can reference one's general feeling about something. Passion is more than just heightened interest, it's a true love for something that you do or something that you follow or have interest in, like the:

- Passion for a favorite sports team

- Passion for the work of a favorite musician, actor, or entertainer

- Passion for a hobby or for other personal interest

- Passion for work or for a business

As you might expect, I will be spending the most time discussing the last of these items, since this is, after all a book on the business of real estate investing. I mention those other things, though, because the same kinds of emotions often apply when it comes to being passionate about something. Having passion for a business pursuit may be something entirely new for you, especially if you've been in work environments that you didn't really enjoy. That said, passion is not just something that you either have or don't have. It can be and should be developed; by doing so, you will only create more income and success as an investor.

First off, how can you tell that you are passionate about something? I think this question can be answered in several ways, perhaps through a few of these telltale signs that passion is what you are experiencing:

- Seeing or discussing something that immediately makes you happier

- That something taps into your emotional side

- Discussion of something that gets you excited and energizes you

- Your heart rate goes up a little bit

- You look forward to (and even plan for) when you get to do or see something

- You love the idea of sharing that something with other people

Let's look at these telltale signs in the context of something you may be more familiar with, and then I'll apply the same things to your business so you can immediately see the parallel.

Starting with the example of a sports team, are you happy when you have the opportunity to see your favorite team play? Do you get emotional during games in which your team plays? Do you love talking about your team to other people, whether they are fans of the team or not? Does watching your team get your blood going a little bit? Do you make plans to see your team play, even if it's just on TV? Do you want to share with the world and with anyone who will watch or listen that you are a fan? If you can answer yes to some or all of these questions, then it's safe to say that you are passionate about your favorite sports team.

There is a significant difference between interest and passion. Interest is a more passive, an unemotional attachment to something. Passion is much deeper. Using the example of the sports fan, a lot of people are interested in sports teams but comparatively few are passionate about them. Business works in much the same way.

A lot of people are interested in business. Ask 100 people if they would like to own a small business (i.e., to be their own boss). A majority would probably like the idea and would say they are interested in it. Ask the same 100 people if they are passionate enough about it to change their professional lives to do it, and you'll likely see that interest drop off considerably. Passion is an extra gear that goes beyond simple interest, and there's just more to it. So where does it come from?

Think about it this way. If you are passionate about a sports team, how did you get to be that way? You weren't born with it. You probably weren't taught to be that way. It may have come from seeing other passionate fans and experiencing something valuable in how they enjoy their team. In part, you wanted to tap into that energy by being like them, and that's how it starts. Business passion is much the same way. You are much more likely to develop a passion for what you do by seeing other investors with passion describe what they do and how they feel about their profession. In short, such energy can be infectious and can help instill that business passion in you.

Beyond where you get your inspiration, passion must be nurtured and developed just like the business itself. Why are you passionate? What is your mission? What is it you most love about the business? What part of us does business bring out that you most love to see? These are the elements of business passion that you must understand and embrace for passion to be something that you truly have for real estate investing or any other business. When you can demonstrate passion, others will see it and also become motivated as a result. Much like a passionate sports fan or movie buff, others who witness true passion may not fully understand it but will admire the conviction and emotion that is behind it. In the context of business, this can be a powerful credibility booster.

Passion can be reflected by exuberant discussion and giving off that intangible vibe that you truly care about what you are doing. That is the purest form of passion for your business. When your passion is based on the love of the process, this will contribute to your ongoing success. For example, when you love interacting with clients, seeing their faces when you are able to present a solution to them, watching a distressed property become something better, and love seeing everyone win in the end, that is true passion for what it means to be an ultimate real estate investor. When you love these things and it shows, you demonstrate a true passion. People will respond to that.

On the flip side of true passion is passion that is misguided. Make no mistake about it; passion for a business and what you are doing is different from passion for making money. I have heard many investors who stated that money was their passion and that was why they loved this business. That is, in my opinion, a recipe for failure in the long run. If you truly love what you do and the foundational elements of your business, the money part will take care of itself. Falling in love with the outcome steals your focus from the important things you need to be doing to get there and, at some point, will be apparent to those around you. In short, true passion for your business is seen as exactly what it is and will generally be admired by those who witness it. Passion for the outcome (in this case, making money) is often seen as something more sinister, something called greed. Be careful about what your passion is based on, because others will see it and may judge you accordingly.

I'm going to throw a curveball your way. I just described the elements of what it means to be passionate and how this can apply favorably to your pursuits as a real estate investor. Now, I'm going to put the brakes on just a bit and encourage you to be cautious about it. Say what? Let me explain.

Passion, for all its benefits, can backfire if it disrupts the balance of what may be an otherwise healthy lifestyle. Passion for sports can be great in some regards, but ask the significant others of avid sports fans and see what their take is on that passion. Ask those same people what they think of their spouses or partners burning the midnight oil on work-related stuff and never having time for the family. Ask them how much they enjoy their partners talking about nothing but business, no matter how excited they are about it. I think you see where I'm going with this. No business is worth alienating those close to you or putting your marriage at risk. Sure, there will be busy times with your business. Just make an effort to keep it real, and your friends and families will appreciate you even more for that than for your passion.

BRIAN'S JOURNAL ENTRY

*"Don't Let Your Passion Interfere
With Your Relationships."*

I'm a very lucky man. I have a beautiful wife, Danielle, who loves and respects me and is there for me through thick and thin. She and I met in seventh grade. She was my first kiss and I was hers. We were so young but crazy in love, I can remember it like it was yesterday. We used to write to each other and pass notes in the hallway and even one of my teachers referred to us as Romeo and Juliet. Unfortunately, at the end of that school year, I had to move away with my family. Danielle and I continued writing and stayed in touch. We'd talk every month or so. Whenever I'd come back to visit, I would look her up and get together. We dated other people growing up, but always had that special connection. Approximately 12 years later, we fell in love again. Two years after that, I asked her to marry me.

Yes, it's a cute story and yes, I still have all the love notes she wrote me in seventh grade. I tell you this story because it is extremely important that you don't let your passion for real estate investing and business success interfere with the love in your relationships. Danielle knows that to me work is not "work." And sometimes she has to tell me to turn off my brain for a while. I'll be honest, it is hard to do sometimes, because the wheels are always turning. But I respect her and I listen to her and she helps keep me in check. So when you are working on your business, work as hard as you can but know that it is just as important to turn it off for a while each day so you don't let your passion interfere with your relationships.

Know that passion can and will serve you well in many areas of your life, including your pursuits of real estate investments. Your team will appreciate your passion and so will your clients. The passion is, in part, what helps establish your credibility and makes people excited about working with you, but you need to have a life, too. There's nothing wrong with working hard and loving what you do. It's sometimes hard, though, to flip off that switch and get out of "business mode" when it is appropriate to do so. For each of you, finding that balance between business and your personal life will be a little bit different. There's no magic formula for how to do it, I just encourage you to strive for balance and in doing so, and you can indeed have your cake and eat it, too.

CHAPTER 7

The Appearance of an Ultimate Real Estate Investor

I would like to have a little bit of fun with this chapter, but don't get me wrong. The issue of your appearance is something you want to care about. The reason is that in all my years as an investor, I've seen some very interesting approaches to this. With all of the different backgrounds you may have experienced before real estate, it's a great chance to set the record straight on how I believe a real estate investor should present himself or herself, appearance-wise.

First and foremost you need to know that there is no situation where appearance is more important than your first impression with someone. Remember "You shouldn't judge a book by its cover"? Well, that doesn't really matter too much these days because that's exactly what people do, and I am just as guilty as you are. However you decide to dress on a regular basis is up to you, just make sure that your first impression with someone with whom you plan to do business is one that will promote rather than discourage future business.

For starters, let's discuss the four main categories of a real estate investor that you can identify by their appearance. Trust me, go to most any REIA meeting and you will see what I am talking about here. I'm not intending undue criticism. If you look in the mirror and say, "Hey, he just described me. What gives?", I'm just compiling years of observation into a general guideline, so go along with me on this and enjoy. Let me list the categories and then elaborate a little on each.

Category 1: The Shameless Pro

Category 2: The Average Joe

Category 3: The Perpetual Wall Streeter

Category 4: The Focused Entrepreneur

Again, there's no right or wrong here. My opinions are just that, and let's just call it a combination of experience and an author's prerogative.

CATEGORY 1: THE SHAMELESS PRO

I refer to this type of individual in a little bit of a sarcastic sense because the so-called shameless pro just never knows when he or she is going to be on a job site or in a more professional setting. You have probably seen the type I'm talking about. Your local REIA holds a meeting and a few guys show up, looking like they just finished a full day of hanging drywall. What's the tendency here? It's not, "Hey honey, look at those guys," nose-in-the-air kind of response. Rather, it's a tendency to want to give them your card to see if they want more work. This would be fine if they were contractors looking to drum up business. It is another if they are fellow investors, because they don't exactly look the part.

There's absolutely nothing wrong with being handy or getting your hands dirty for some of your deals. That said, when it comes to meeting with clients or with team members, you also don't want to appear like you just left a job site. Not only does it suggest you have a bit much on your plate, but it also does not present an overall professional image. Clients want to see that you know how to handle their situation rather than be the person an investor would hire to fix up their properties for them. To each their own, but remember you never get a second chance to make a first impression. I suggest you make the most of that opportunity.

CATEGORY 2: THE AVERAGE JOE

The Average Joe, often accompanied by Average Jane, is one of the most common looks you'll see at meetings of investors. There's nothing specifically wrong with this approach, and it's probably not something that's given a whole lot of thought by people around them. Which is precisely my point. The Average Joe does a fabulous job of blending in with the crowd and is probably a decent-enough person to interact with. He is also entirely unmemorable, especially if he is quiet and doesn't say much.

A big part of the networking game is to stand out among other people and be positively memorable. Whether it's attire or, more important, what you say and do, you want people to remember who you are. The Average Joes, because of their tendency to blend in with their surroundings, must work extra hard to network and have people remember who they are. Their ability to blend is by and large a virtue of their casual dress, and many investors who fit this category are also newbies. They may wish to blend in because they are new and are nervous about having to interact with people in a profession they don't know much about yet. As long as they are able to eventually come out of their shells and be more noticeable, this is an OK way to start.

On the flip side, the nondescript nature of the Average Joes makes it easy for them to fit in and interact with clients. What they may lack in knowledge (for the less-experienced investor), they make up for with natural rapport, and they tend to be able to put clients at ease better than the Wall Streeter or even the entrepreneur. Basically, they're just being themselves, and as long as they can convey the message at hand, this look is actually a pretty good recipe for success.

CATEGORY 3: THE PERPETUAL WALL STREETER

This REIA meeting classic is almost always someone you'll see in groups of investors. No matter how casual the setting, there's always some guy (no intentional gender bias here, but the person in question is usually a man) who shows up in a pressed suit, tie, and the cufflinks to match. This choice of apparel is great if there's an unscheduled board meeting, but this is an investor meeting, so let's keep it real. I've seen people dressed like this at REIA meetings and, admittedly, my first thought is, "OK, at what point are they going to stand up and try to sell something?" Maybe I'm incorrect in thinking that, but first impressions are what they are.

Here's my recommendation. Keep the suit and tie for when you really need it. Neither other investors nor your clients are really going to expect that you dress so formally, and it's going to look funny more so than it will impress people. That hits on a good point. The perpetual Wall Streeter is most likely donning Armani to impress his peers rather than for any other purpose. Nice attire is fine, but it shouldn't be what draws attention to you. Ultimately, what you say and do is most important and that should be the focus of those around you, rather than what you are wearing.

CATEGORY 4: THE FOCUSED ENTREPRENEUR

Of all the categories, this is perhaps the one you most want to aspire to become, should you decide that a subtle wardrobe shift or change of look is warranted. The entrepreneur is out there for one purpose and that is to do deals. They also carry a fierce independent spirit and have disdain for the status quo. Appearance-wise, the entrepreneur may feature a modest amount of so-called bling, like a nice watch, but not overdo it by any stretch. He or she is likely (by the numbers) to be an expatriated member of corporate America and may show independence through a strict avoidance of suits and ties.

In short, the phrase "casual but nice" will often apply to the appearance of the entrepreneur. Nice pants or jeans, some type of shirt with a collar, quality shoes, you get the idea. The entrepreneur exudes a casual confidence by dressing the part. They know that it is not their formal attire but rather their dedicated approach to doing business that will attract people to them, and they are right. Entrepreneurism is about a certain spirit and is tangible enough so that other people notice. When you see this type of individual, give him or her a card and have a conversation. These are often the real movers and shakers out there and are usually good people to know. Their influence still has to be proven, as with anybody, but the way they generally carry themselves is a good start.

Beyond the basic categories, I want to discuss a few things regarding your appearance that will be of immense help to you as you attempt to establish and grow your business. No one type of attire is perfect for all situations. If you have a client who is a banker who is meeting during lunch, you don't necessarily have to put on a suit, but do make an effort to dress the part and appear a more professional. That's what they will be used to seeing and most likely will be expecting.

On the flip side, if you are meeting a client who lives in the country, a more casual approach is probably advisable. Show up in a suit in this situation and the client may think you're there to sell encyclopedias.

BRIAN'S KEY POINT

When you match clients in terms of your appearance, they will see themselves as being more like you. This establishes a silent level of rapport and can go a long way toward your success.

ADDITIONAL COMMENTS REGARDING YOUR
APPEARANCE AND MATERIAL ITEMS

- Ties: You're neither attending a board meeting nor a funeral so, generally speaking, leave the ties on the tie rack.

- Briefcases: This isn't Wall Street, and a briefcase may be intimidating to some clients. In most cases, a day planner and a simple folder that contains your paperwork will suffice.

- Bling: Whether it's jewelry, gold watches, etc., do your best to match the client and don't overdo it. Your goal is to connect with the clients, not impress them.

- Hats: There aren't many situations in which a hat is at all useful in a business setting, unless you're meeting a client at a tractor pull or on an archaeological dig site.

- Phones: We all have cell phones now, so while it's not unusual to be seen carrying one, leave it out of sight and don't you dare answer it during a meeting. If you do, you could be seen as unprofessional and disrespectful. Oh, and in regards to Bluetooth headsets, don't wear one during a meeting or anytime that you are not on a call. They don't make you look important, they make you look silly.

- Vehicles: You may not have a choice as to what vehicle you use when you show up for a meeting. That said, showing up in a beat-up clunker might indirectly create a poor first impression. Remember, clients want to feel like they can connect with you, and if your ride makes you look poor as dirt then you may want to consider upgrading to something that doesn't draw attention. However, don't stretch yourself in the beginning. Be patient, the BMW will come with time.

What the pundits say about first impressions is dead-on correct when it comes to your success as a real estate investor. Never forget that the investing community has had some bad press in the past few years, and the public's perception of real estate investors may be, at the very least, a little skeptical. Sure, the message you deliver is ultimately the most important thing and can be what helps validate your authority. That said, how you present yourself, appearance-wise, can set the tone (good or bad) in your interaction with a client and can either make your job much easier or much more difficult.

Personally, I prefer for things to be as easy as possible and let others make the business more complicated than it actually is. How you dress and when you show up are simple and yet critical parts of how you communicate who you are to a client and that is an important part of your professionalism. I'm not suggesting that any of you go out there and change your wardrobe just for the sake of your business. Simply strive to convey an image of confidence, success, and experience. This in turn should instill confidence in the client of your ability to get the job done. Business casual should suffice in most situations. Just be mindful of the importance of your appearance, and you'll already be a step ahead of the game.

BRIAN'S JOURNAL ENTRY

"A lesson From My College Baseball Coach"

Not only does your physical appearance affect your first impression with a client, but I must also mention the importance of being on time as well.

I went to a small University and played Division III athletics. I played second base, started all four years, and was elected captain of the team my senior year. Playing baseball was the highlight of my college years.

During this time, my baseball coach always drove a point home to me and my teammates that has stuck with me, and I would like to drive it home to you: "If you're early, you're on time. If you're on time, you're late. If you're late, you're forgotten."

It's short and sweet and also true to any aspect of life, but especially business. It doesn't matter how good you look or how well you are dressed or how smart and well-spoken you are. If you show up late for a commitment, then you may very well ruin any opportunity you might have had with the person stuck waiting on you. Always remember the lesson my baseball coach taught me and make it another arsenal in your weaponry as you strive for success as an ultimate real estate investor.

CHAPTER 8

The Workplace of an Ultimate Real Estate Investor

The old saying goes that a man's home is his castle. Beyond the medieval reference, I think there is still some truth here in the modern era. The home is the most sacred of places where one does not have to put forth your best show, can relax, and enjoy those things unrelated to work or business. That's all well and good, but what happens when a home-based business enters the picture? Things may get a little more complicated and it could affect your performance as an investor, so let's explore the issue of business workplace a little more.

You have a number of options for where you conduct your real estate investing business:

- Dedicated (purchased or leased) office space

- Time-shared office space

- Home-based office

I'll take a moment and discuss some of the issues with each of these options and will then review the essential components of your office, regardless of where it is.

DEDICATED (PURCHASED OR LEASED) OFFICE SPACE

The dedicated office is a great idea for many investors, but is also the most expensive of the options available to you. You'll have to locate space to either rent or purchase, which can be a considerable expense in some areas or at least beyond the scope of a start-up business. Dedicated office space also has no furniture, shelves, etc., and will require separate utilities. All of these things can add up quickly and can be prohibitive for many new business owners, including real estate investors.

The advantage of a dedicated office is that your business has a separate location, making it easier to separate work from home and maintain personal privacy with respect to your team and clients. The latter issue alone is not enough to warrant a dedicated office, as a simple business mailing address is sufficient at first to give your personal life and address the privacy they deserve. Beyond privacy, a dedicated office is clearly a sign of credibility and will be seen as a plus by not only your clients, but team members, too.

There is no need to rush into an office, but in my opinion, it is an essential step at some point if you want to take your real estate business to the highest possible level.

BRIAN'S JOURNAL ENTRY

"Where I Initially Operated My Real Estate Investing Business"

When I began my quest for millionaire real estate success, I worked out of an 8-by-10-foot clutter-filled room in my house, which I designated as my office. I got my desk and file cabinet for free. It was the old steel case stuff that weighed a ton but was virtually indestructible. To be honest, I think that I got the stuff for free because not even the Salvation Army would accept it as a donation. Hell, I accepted it. It was like finding treasure for me because it was free and I needed it.

My office wasn't pretty to look at, but it worked! I set up and organized my little file system, had a marker board on my wall, had a map of my city on my wall, and so on. I was hell-bent on making it work. For the first two years of my existence as a real estate investor, I worked from this office in my home. I would meet with potential sellers and buyers at one of my many local offices around town: Starbucks, Arby's, McDonald's, and other choice locations. My system worked, but for me personally, something was missing. It was hard to work from home. I was beginning to close some pretty big deals and make some good money, but working from home was difficult.

I eventually realized that the reason working from home was hard on me was because it was difficult for me to turn off my working brain in the evenings and focus my attention to my wife. Working from home turned out to be a double-edged sword because when I was at home, I was at work, and when I was at work, I was at home. At times, I felt trapped. One day I realized that it was time to push the envelope and go to the next level. That next level was renting office space and setting up a location to operate my business outside of my home.

I remember it like it was yesterday. It was very scary for me to do this, but I had to face this fear and give it a shot; otherwise, I knew deep down that my business would never grow to its full potential.

Looking back now, that was one of the best decisions I ever made. It wasn't like flipping a switch with instant results, but it did slowly fuel the fire in my business and in me personally. It was just the change I needed to take me to the next level.

If the move to a dedicated office seems warranted, congratulations! This decision is most likely based on a need that is fueled by a certain volume of business. Basically, it should be a sign that things are going well. When the time is right to move to a dedicated office, you'll probably know and should have the revenue to support the move.

TIME-SHARED OFFICE SPACE

A newer office concept that is gaining popularity is called a time-shared office space. Here's how it works. You lease the right to use office space at a particular location for certain blocks of time each week. In some cases, you can also pay a set fee and schedule the space when you need it, say for meetings or conference calls. This can offer the appearance of a dedicated office but without the cost and headache of having to manage it all yourself. As a real estate investor who will likely not need a full-time office right out of the gate this may be a good option to consider. It also displays professionalism by having a formal meeting place to offer clients that isn't in a coffee shop.

The downside to this option is that the other renters at these part-time offices are usually not given storage space, so don't plan on being able to store all your files and equipment there. You'll have the flexibility of office space, but likely will still need office space at home for the rest of your business needs.

HOME-BASED OFFICE

The home-based office is where I originally started and is, without a doubt, the most common starting place for the beginning real estate investor. There is no need to purchase or lease an office and it will require far less capital to equip the office when it is at home. Spare or reconfigured bedrooms are probably the most common locations for home offices, followed by finished basements and nooks or extra spaces in an existing room. The latter is the only one I really don't favor, although I recognize that, for some readers, this may be the best current option.

When considering where to set up your home office, the following needs are all relevant:

- Peace and quiet, because you will spend time on the phone in your office

- Storage space for your equipment, files, and paperwork

- Uninterrupted access to computers and the Internet

- Lack of potential distractions (TV, barking dog, crying child, etc.)

I recognize that a home office is often something of an intrusion to the space and time dynamic for you and your family, but you really need to be able to make or take calls when necessary and be able to access your computer at a moment's notice, so consider these things carefully. Having to go outside to do your calls or wait until your child is done surfing the Internet before you can use the computer, in the absence of a Plan B, will get old real quick.

At this time, you may also be wondering how to conduct client meetings when you work from home. Should you meet with them at your home office? I wouldn't recommend it. Privacy is very important, and you'll be surprised how nosy some clients can be. Instead, set up meetings at any one of your many local offices such as Starbucks, McDonald's, and Wendy's. If anyone asks why you are meeting there, be honest. Say that you work from home and that you like to keep your business life separate from your personal life. This is not uncommon nowadays, and as a result, people will and should respect your honesty.

Workplace Pros & Cons

	Pro's	Con's
Dedicated Office	Great place for client meetings Increased professional credibility Best option if you have employees Easier to separate work life from home life Flexibility with the look of your office space More exposure for your business depending on the location	Monthly lease payment for space Monthly utilities for space Travel time to and from home Have to furnish space yourself
Time-Shared Office	OK place for meetings Increased professional credibility Easier to separate work life from home life Ability to share some office space overhead cost with other tenants Space already furnished	Monthly lease payment for space Monthly utilities for space Travel time to and from home Less flexibility with what you can and can't do with the space No storage space for your things
Home-Based Office	Low monthly overhead No commute to and from work	Easy to get distracted at home Easy to procrastinate at home Unable to hold client meetings Inconvenient for employees Difficult to separate work life from home life Less perceived credibility with some clients

ESSENTIAL OFFICE COMPONENTS

Regardless of your office location, your place of doing business for your real estate investing will require a few essentials. While not all-inclusive, I have listed the most important things you'll need based on my experiences:

- Computer, desktop or laptop (personally, I prefer a Mac)

- A dedicated work desk

- High-speed Internet access

- Mobile phone with plenty of minutes

- Local phone line

- Business cards

- Organized and readily available forms and paperwork

- Printer (color is ideal)

- Fax machine (one that can also scan is ideal)

- A dedicated business mailing address (PO box or UPS box)

- A dedicated e-mail account. Stick with a non-business account like john@yahoo.com rather than a john@webuyhouses.com account because: (1) It is free. (2) I've found it to be less intimidating for a distressed homeowner. (3) There may be times when negotiating with mortgage institutions that you would prefer to be viewed as an individual person rather than an investment company.

- Business Web site

- Accounting software

- File organization capacity for different projects and deals

Note that the list above does not include basic office supplies, as I think the need for these should be apparent.

OTHER HELPFUL TIPS

To help with the proper balance between your business and personal life, I suggest having dedicated business hours. I appreciate that the business of being an investor can sometimes spill into the evenings and weekends – and I'm not suggesting leaving these times off limits – but have some definition as to how your time is spent. For example, if you typically find the afternoons during any given week to be pretty slow, don't take calls during that time. Rather, return calls at a defined time in the evening. You'll be more apt to reach clients then and won't feel like you're a slave to your phone. Accessibility is one thing, and being consumed by your business is another. I believe in a happy medium.

A well-constructed Web site can also help alleviate worries that you'll potentially lose business during your down time. Visitors can learn about you, submit inquiries, and request to visit with you during your normal office hours. The ability to set hours when you are working your business is not only healthy but also helps you to appear more like a retail business that has set hours. This is especially helpful if you start the business as a part-time venture.

Let me emphasize that I'm not suggesting that anyone go out and lease or purchase dedicated office space for your real estate investing business even if that may become more relevant and necessary later. The most important thing you need right out of the gate is some dedicated place from which to conduct business. I recognize that this may be challenging for many readers. You may not have that finished basement or spare bedroom that could serve as an office. In these cases, all you can do is the best you can.

Remember, too, the important issue of balance between life and business. A future as a real estate investor can be very exciting but also somewhat consuming. Between meetings, phone calls, and time online doing research, the business (like any) has the potential to blur the line between your home life and work, especially when the business is home-based. Make the effort to find that right balance, and in the long run, you will be much happier and able to truly enjoy the fruits of your business from the comfort of home.

The importance of a physical office is much less of an issue for either your professional team or for your clients. You of course will be going to meet them in most cases and you are more important than the perception of where your actual business is located. Your true business results will come from who you are in the eyes of those who will be evaluating you. The bottom line is, just get started at home and then work your way to an external office only if that is your desire and only if revenue can support the move.

BRIAN'S KEY POINT

Worry about making lots of money first before worrying about making lots of changes.

CHAPTER 9

Holding Client Meetings as an Ultimate Real Estate Investor

It is safe to say, now, that you are well on your way to being more informed about the reality of operating a real estate investing business. I have covered much of the basic mindset, skills, and traits that you need to have and now would like to move to a sequence of chapters addressing the operational aspects of your business.

Operations in real estate investing include things like client relations, customer service, transactional processing, accounting, and fundraising. Since these factors are critical to the growth and stability of your business, they are worth mentioning on their foundational merit alone.

Let's start by discussing the important and necessary meetings that you will be having with clients. Meetings with clients occur frequently in this business, and it should not surprise you that these meetings will largely reflect your professionalism. Some of the basic kinds of meetings you will experience on a regular basis include:

- Meetings with sellers

- Meetings with prospective buyers

- Meetings with team members

- Meetings with business partners

BRIAN'S JOURNAL ENTRY

"How I Initially Met With Clients"

In my early days, I did not have this luxury. But now that I operate my business out of a physical office space, I always first meet with clients by having them come to me. I do this for three reasons: (1) Convenience for me, as it is time-consuming and cumbersome to always have to leave your place of work to go meet a new client at their home or at a fast-food restaurant, although I did do it this way in the beginning and there was nothing wrong with it at all. (2) When clients come to me and see my office and all of the testimonial letters on my conference room wall, it demonstrates a level of credibility and that I am serious about what I do and can potentially work with them, too. (3) Lastly, by having new clients come to me first at my office, it creates a level of authority and respect for me. New prospects must be willing to meet at my office on my terms or likely not meet at all for these three reasons. And the good news is, it works perfectly for me and usually works perfectly for my clients.

Since you are operating a dynamic business, one in which two of your workdays are likely never going to be exactly alike, it is hard to point to a single strategy for each kind of meeting that will work for you each and every time. The moving target nature of real estate investing makes it a very exciting business to be in, but can also make it challenging to get accustomed to, especially when you are new to the business. For this reason, I will discuss each of the mentioned meeting types and what you should be trying to do to get the best outcome and results from your efforts.

MEETINGS WITH SELLERS

When most real estate investors think of meetings, they will envision going to a new property and seeing if it meets their criteria for a profitable deal. This breeds natural excitement and also some apprehension, especially when one is new to the business. I think a very common pitfall for the novice investor is putting too much pressure on oneself when meeting with sellers. This isn't rocket science. Take it easy on yourself and not only will your stress level go down, but also your meetings will be more productive.

The tendency is for the novice investor to think he or she must try to ink the deal on the spot during that initial meeting with a client. Does this happen? Sure it does, but you don't need to put pressure on yourself to make it happen each time. Let's review some of the basics with a little quiz:

YOUR PRIMARY MISSION IN A MEETING WITH A SELLER IS TO:

    a. Gather information

    b. Get a feeling for how motivated they are

    c. Develop good rapport with the client

    d. All of the above

As you might expect, the correct answer is d, all of the above. Your primary mission is not to ink a deal, although if circumstances call for it, you should always be ready as this is your number-one objective. In the majority of other cases, your mission should be to learn what is going on, why they may be motivated to do something, and make yourself positively memorable to the client. When you do these things, each and every time, your meetings will be a success, and you will also spend far less time and energy worrying about trying to get contracts signed on the spot.

Please note here that I am not openly discouraging you from being expeditious about getting good deals put to contract, because time is often of the essence for the great deals that are out there. Don't spend so much time thinking about inking a deal that you lose sight of the other important parts of a successful meeting with a seller.

You can perhaps thank the real estate trainers out there for making everyone think they should always be Johnny on the spot when it comes to working with sellers. I simply find that good communication is a constant and better focus for you as you are getting started. As you grow in this business, opportunities to act on the spot will appear. Be patient and don't fall into the trap of thinking it works like that all the time, because it just isn't so. Many of your best deals will come from following up and patiently working a deal rather than trying to be unnecessarily pushy. You also will be viewed as more respectful if sellers don't feel you're trying to rush them into a decision they may need some time to think about.

BRIAN'S KEY POINT

Time and circumstances often change people's minds, so always leave the door open for future business.

TOP SECRET WHAT-TO-SAY SCRIPTS FOR BUYING HOUSES

Talking with sellers and buyers and knowing what to say and why can be a very intimidating part of the business; however, the intimidation can be overcome with practice. Whatever you do, don't let the fear of not knowing what to say stop you. Simply gather information and present offers.

INTRODUCTION SCRIPTS

- "I have a few ideas in mind on how I can buy your house. First of all, I want you to know that I am an investor and I need to find a way to make a profit or else I have no reason to get involved. I'm sure that you can understand that."

- "Hi (first name), you called on my ad, and you probably know that I don't plan to live in your house, correct? I am looking to make a profit on your house at (address), and I will do that in a way that hopefully will get you what you want, too. My profit will come from my new buyer or tenant, and I'm sure you understand that if I can't make a profit then I really don't have any reason to get involved. Does that make sense?"

- "The main way I buy houses is by taking over debt on a property, making payments to a seller on a property, or by paying cash. But the only way that I pay cash is at a discount."

- "How much are you looking to get out of this thing?"

- "What is the least you will take?"

- "Will you sell for what you owe on it?"

  - If yes, consider moving forward with subject-to or seller financing

  - If no:

    - "What is the least you would take if I paid you cash for your equity and take over your loan quickly?"

    - "Is that the best you can do?"

    - "So you're saying that if you don't get X then you won't sell me your house?"

- "Will you allow me to make payments to you for the home?"

SUBJECT-TO SCRIPTS

- "OK (first name), after reviewing the information you gave me, I have good news. It looks like I can buy your house and close within a few days. There are a few different ways that I buy houses, and my number one way is that I take over your payments and start making them when you and I agree, and I'll continue to do so until your loan is paid off sometime in the future. I'll even pay for your closing costs so you can move whenever you're ready. But the only way that I can buy it is if the loan stays in your name until I pay it off. Will that keep you awake at night?"

- "If I come out to look at your house and like what I see, are you (and your spouse) ready to sell the house today and get the paperwork done while I'm there?"

- "The loan will actually be good on your credit, because I will be making the payments and keeping it in good standing."

- "As soon as you sell me this house, I don't want you to ever worry about it again."

- "Mr./Ms. (name), since I will be taking over your payments and putting my own money into this property, I will need to have ownership, because I never put money in a home that I don't own. I'm sure you can understand that."

SELLER-FINANCING SCRIPTS

- "OK (first name), I usually wouldn't take a deal like this because your house doesn't quite meet my cash-buying criteria; however, if you can wait a little while to collect the amount you are asking, then I'll make an exception. If I like what I see, I'll buy your house now and close with an attorney when you're ready. I'll pay you your equity in monthly payments so you can move and put this house behind you now. How does that sound?"

- "Well, let me ask you this. If we could come to an agreement on price, would you be willing to wait for your equity or do you have to have everything now?"

- If the seller requests interest:

  - "Interest; I wasn't basing my purchase amount on paying interest. My plan was simply to pay you monthly based on an amount that you and I agree. Also, if I pay you interest, you'll have to pay taxes on that; are you sure you need interest?"

- If seller still insists on interest:

  - "OK, what interest rate did you have in mind?"

  - "Is that the best you can do?"

  - "So you're saying that unless you get X% interest, you won't sell me the house?"

OPTION-TO-PURCHASE SCRIPT

- "OK (first name), I told you that I had a few ideas in mind on how I can buy your house. The other thing I can offer you is for me to 'option' your house for an amount that you and I would agree on and pay you cash for that amount. But before I bring my money to the table, I am going to find my new buyer to come in and buy the house from me so I can find a way to make a profit. So basically what I would do is option your house, then I'll need a little time to spend my money and time and resources to find someone to buy it from me. Once I find my buyer, we can go to the attorney and close and you can be out of this thing. In the meantime, you are obviously going to continue to make your payments. There is no risk to you whatsoever. If I can't find my buyer, then you are in no worse position than you are in right now. You get what you want, and I make my money based on finding my buyer, not by charging any fees or commissions. How does that sound?"

SHORT-SALE SCRIPT

- "OK (first name), despite the fact that you are behind in payments, I am still very interested in buying your house and, in turn, stopping foreclosure. Basically, in order for me to buy in this situation I'll be buying from you but negotiating with your lender in an attempt to get them to take a discount on the mortgage balance so I can buy the property with some equity. The reason your lender would even consider a discount is because they know that their only alternative is to foreclose and likely take back the home, which is definitely not something they want to deal with. Therefore, it is likely that they would be very willing to entertain an offer from me in this situation. There is no risk or cost to you at all. The only thing I need from you is your full cooperation so that I can get the lender what they need and in turn try to buy your house before a foreclosure sale. How does that sound?"

ADDITIONAL SCRIPTS (SUBJECT-TO AND SELLER-FINANCE)

- "OK (first name), you're asking _____ for a house that you say is worth _____. I don't see any way that I can make a profit unless we can create some kind of financing here that will allow me to make money. And the only way I can do that is, first of all, I have to get a price at least a little below absolute top retail value. Secondly, you are asking for _____ money down, and frankly, I can't give you _____ money down on a house worth_____ and be able to make a profit. Because the truth is, what I intend to do is put an owner occupant in the house, and shortly thereafter, get them to the point where they will get a new loan on the property and cash us both out at the same time."

- "I'll take over your debt, and I'll pay you _____ when I cash out, and you will be secured with a second mortgage on the house with no payments and no interest. You'll get paid when I get paid, and in the meantime, you can forget about the house. Isn't that fair?"

- "Your payments will be made and you can forget about the house until you get a call saying the loan was paid off."

- "The note will be recorded and secured against the house. You are protected because I can't sell the house until I pay you off first."

POTENTIAL SELLER OBJECTIONS

How do I know I can trust you?

- "Well, have I given you any reason to believe that you can't trust me? If you feel that selling your house to me will keep you awake at night, then perhaps you shouldn't do the deal. The fact is, unless it is a win-win situation, then I don't want to get involved."

How long have you been doing this?

- "I've been doing this for _____ (years/months) now, and my number-one goal is to buy properties where I can find a way to make a profit and put food on my family's table and give the seller what he or she needs at the same time. If you are interested in selling, then I am interested in buying."

What if you don't do what you say you'll do?

- "Well, if I don't do what I say I'll do, then I surely can't find a way to make a profit. I plan to do what I say, which is why our transaction will be closed with my attorney."

Why don't I just list the property with a Realtor?

- "Your welcome to do that, but I'm not a Realtor. Your reason for listing a property would be to find a buyer, and you've got one right here. So unless you can afford to wait it out and pay commissions and closing costs if and when your Realtor does find you a buyer, then perhaps we should move forward now. The bottom line is you should do what you feel is in your best interest."

What do you charge?

- "I don't charge any fees, commissions – nothing – and in fact when I close, there is a very good possibility that I can pay all your closing costs as well."

I'd like to have my attorney review this deal.

- "Sure, not a problem. Is there something that you would like me to go over with you again to clarify? Also, is there something that you would want your attorney to advise you on? Remember, we'll close with my attorney anyway, so everything is handled professionally at all times."

What if your new tenant or buyer messes up the house?

- "That wouldn't be your problem, it would be mine. I wouldn't worry about that because I don't find renters, I find people that want to be homeowners. In fact, they are typically fixing up the home and not trashing it, but that is a fair question."

MEETINGS WITH PROSPECTIVE BUYERS

Meetings with prospective buyers are very exciting, as sales usually are what put money directly in your pocket. I suggest a few guidelines that will help you manage these kinds of meetings and also make them as productive as possible.

First, prescreen your buyer prospects over the phone. Untold time is wasted by investors showing properties to buyer prospects who are marginally or even poorly qualified. Especially now with tighter mortgage rules, you just can't afford to drive across town to show a property twice a day to marginal buyers. Ultimately, there are only two things you need to know about buyers to determine immediately if they are a prospect or a suspect. They must have money and/or credit. If a buyer has money, then you can consider a lease option. If a buyer has credit, then you can consider getting him or her a conventional loan. If the buyer has neither, then there is virtually nothing you can do for him or her at this time.

In regards to letting buyers see your properties, you also have two options. First, you can put a lock box on the front door and give people the code to go inside and view the property at their convenience. Second, you can drive out to the property and show the home to every Dick, Jane, and Sally who wants to see it. For me, the decision is easy. I've never shown a house and don't plan to because it is not worth my time. I would much rather let prospective buyers show themselves in and out without me being there. You're allowed to disagree with me on this subject, but before you do, I recommend you try this system (which is exactly what it is, a system) before you completely knock it. If it is going to keep you awake at night wondering if someone might steal something, then don't do it. Again, what is the worst that can happen? If they steal the fridge (the odds are against it), so what? I've never had anyone steal anything of value from any of my houses.

BRIAN'S JOURNAL ENTRY

"Actually, Something Did Get Stolen."

OK, I confess that there was one house from which someone stole some things. What was stolen were some brand-new plug-in air fresheners that we had just put in a house we were trying to sell on a rent-to-own.

I have to be honest, I was a little annoyed by that, but hey, if that is the only thing that gets stolen, then I think I'm doing fine.

Listen, I've done hundreds of deals and in that amount of time, the only thing being stolen were some air fresheners, well, that's not too darn bad if you ask me.

Long story short, my experience is that most people are not likely to steal anything. If they do steal anything of major value, that is why we have insurance. Your time and sanity are worth more than anything that could reasonably be stolen.

So why operate this way? Well, aside from saving you hours and hours of time that you can apply to generating more business, believe it or not, it relays a sense of integrity with the way you conduct business. People appreciate the ability to view a property without someone breathing down their necks. Believe me when I tell you that nothing says, "I'm desperate to sell this place," like you herding clients through a property and asking them if they like it 5 or 10 times. Clients are going to make their own decisions, so just let them do their thing. After they've seen the house, all I ask is that they call and let me know that they have locked the house. At that time, I find out what they think. If they like it, then we meet and reach an initial agreement. If they don't, then I just saved hours of wasted time. Buyers like this system and feel a strong sense of initial trust with you, because you are showing professionalism and trust to them.

Lastly, don't be afraid to call these buyers to action. This means scheduling a meeting with them and ultimately collecting a good faith deposit. Take the bull by the horns, handle the follow-up proactively, and your success will increase. The follow-up aspect, a subject of a later chapter, also displays to others that you take this seriously and will act accordingly.

TOP SECRET WHAT-TO-SAY-SCRIPT FOR SELLING HOUSES

Selling houses is a lot less intimidating for most real estate investors, which is why the scripts in this section are shorter and less complex. Typically, you are going to sell houses one of four ways: (1) lease option, (2) seller financing, (3) wholesale, or (4) retail to an owner-occupant getting a new loan.

- "Now that I have your information, the next step is for you to go out and look at the home. If you like what you see, then we'll get together to get the paperwork done and secure your spot as first in line for the home."

- "Our homes are sold on a first-come, first-served basis, and since we make it easy for people to buy, they usually don't last that long on the market. So if you are interested at all, then I would strongly suggest that we get together sooner rather than later."

BUYER FAQS

How does your financing work?

- "We offer owner financing where we can sell you the home without you having to qualify at a bank."

How much down payment do I need?

- "We are very flexible with down payment. We can offer you many options, and we will always do our best to work with whatever funds you have available. You can even start out on a lease-purchase and then move to owner financing at a later date when you have the additional money."

Do you offer down payment assistance programs?

- "Yes, we do. A lot of times if you are a bit short on the down payment, we can set up a monthly payment plan spread out over 6 to 12 months."

What other methods of down payment are accepted?

- "Unlike most lending institutions, we accept borrowed funds for closing. If you have a close friend or relative willing to lend you money for your down payment, you can use that in our program. You may also be eligible to withdraw or borrow from your 401(k) to purchase a home without penalties. We also accept trades, such as other real estate, automobiles, etc."

How does your lease-purchase program work?

- "We can lease you the home with the exclusive right to purchase it at a later date. Our buyers love it because it gives them time to save up for a larger down payment, time to clean up past credit problems, time to sell another home, and also time to try out the neighborhood before buying. We are obligated to sell to you; however, you are not obligated to buy. One-hundred percent of your option fee or down payment is credited toward the purchase price of the home."

What is the interest rate on your owner financing?

- "We are flexible with our terms to meet your needs. Our typical interest rates range from 7.5% to 9.5% depending on down payment and application. All credit is considered and applications are necessary to verify income and employment."

I love the home, what is the next step?

- "All we need is your application, which can be downloaded from our Web site if you don't have one already. You can even fax it in for faster processing. We will then contact you within 24 hours once we verify income and employment. Please keep in mind that our homes sell quickly, so time is of the essence."

TOP 10 REASONS WHY A LEASE-TO-OWN
PROGRAM IS ATTRACTIVE TO BUYERS

1. No banks to deal with: No more bank hassles!

2. Own your own home: You enjoy the benefits of owning your own home before you technically ever buy it!

3. Improving your property: Because you will own this property soon, any improvements you do that increase the value of the home allow you to build more equity yourself.

4. Flexibility: You have total flexibility and the option to buy your home, not an obligation.

5. Your credit: You are creating a strong credit reference while you are leasing-to-own. We have a credit-repair assistance programs to help you clean up the past for good.

6. Rent credits: Potential rent credits may be available each month. Imagine a chunk of your rent going to the purchase of your home, allowing you to build equity in your home faster than a traditional mortgage – no more wasting money on rent.

7. Down payment in installments: If you don't have the 10% to 20% down that a bank typically requires, then we'll allow you to pay in your down payment over time and based on your comfort level.

8. Work for equity: Often we'll forgo a big chunk of the option deposit if you do some improvements to the house. This allows you to get in light and create equity up front.

9. Will accept trades: Say you don't have enough money up front for the deposit, that's OK because we can accept other forms of down payment, such as other real estate, a car, a boat, a motorcycle, stocks, bonds, etc. We decided to offer this program to our clients because we believe in being flexible, unlike a bank or mortgage company.

10. Immediate occupancy: Many times we can offer immediate occupancy with our homes when doing a lease-to-own.

MEETINGS WITH TEAM MEMBERS

Meetings with team members are less frequent than other meetings, but are no less important. I think these are some of the easiest meetings to work with, because you can have a set agenda and expect that it can be followed with little deviation. For example, you schedule a meeting with your Realtor to discuss a new market niche you want to pursue. While you aren't exactly sure what the meeting will produce as a result, you should have a pretty clear idea of what you are going to talk about, making the meeting move along smoothly.

When meeting with team members, let them know in advance the purpose for the meeting and how long you expect it will last. This is referred to as the meeting before the meeting. Ultimately, if you want your meetings to be successful, then the appropriate parties should know what to expect. This allows them to prepare and is respectful of their busy schedules. As far as meeting conduct goes, be sure you are on time and, minus a little friendly chit-chat, keep things on task so nobody feels like their time is being wasted. I also suggest summarizing the meeting when it ends so that everyone knows what their next steps are, answering the question "So, where do we go from here?" When you can do these basic things, your professionalism as a goal-oriented and organized entrepreneur will shine through and impress your team members.

MEETINGS WITH BUSINESS PARTNERS

Some of you have formal business partners, some of you are married to your business partners, and some of you may simply be considering whether or not a partner is right for you. For many investors, partnerships can be good ways to capitalize on the strengths of the members and should result in more overall productivity. Some partnerships are simple relationships between a financier and an investor for a particular deal. Others are more detailed relationships that affect the business on a more regular basis. Regardless, your meetings with them will have some similarities.

Chances are your association with a business partner has already been at least partially established, so the whole first impression thing is less of an issue. However, if you're in charge of getting something ready for a meeting or have progress to report on, then it is a good idea to have done what you were supposed to do. This is very logical, but is often overlooked. It is wise to make sure partners have proper accountability to each other and that each partner is comfortable with both receiving and giving opinions or criticisms as warranted.

Whatever you do, if you decide to operate with a partner, make sure that you get everything in writing upfront. Each partner should know from the beginning of the partnership what the other person is accountable for. I have seen and been involved in business partnerships that have succeeded and failed. Sadly, partnerships seem to end because one person is doing more than the other, which in turn creates bitterness and hostility. Know your roles and do what you say you are going to do to the best of your ability. Another option you may choose to consider if you are unsure about establishing a long-term partnership is to create a partnership on a deal-by-deal basis. This way you are not locked in to any long-term commitments with anyone. If you can't or don't want to be accountable to anyone, then don't get into a partnership. The good news is that a partner is not necessarily needed for ultimate success in this business.

As you've seen from my little discussion here, meetings in this type of business are critical to your success. Sometimes meetings are cut and dry, right to the point, if you will. Sometimes they are speculative and involve a lot of brainstorming. Sometimes they are a mystery, giving you little advance notice of really what to expect. Regardless, your approach to meetings and ability to handle them will be a huge part of your business arsenal. Treat each and every meeting as if it is worthy of your full and undivided attention, and your various clients will never be left feeling like they were a waste of your valuable time, even if the meeting doesn't end up being as productive as you might have hoped.

The way to approach meetings is a lot like approaching a client for the first time. In an initial meeting, the first impression a client has of you will have a lot of bearing on whether or not they choose to do business with you. Similarly, a scheduled meeting is basically a continuation of that first impression a client had of you. You may have to use a little intuition or gut instinct to gather what their first impression may have been. Beyond that, you have a great opportunity with meetings to either:

- Continue a good relationship that started off on the right foot

- Right the ship if your first encounter with a client ran into some snags

When you are organized, attentive, task-oriented, and just plain personable, the general flow of most meetings will be in your favor. Clients know that you are meeting for a reason and, more often than not, they will be expecting that you will dictate the flow of meetings. Be prepared to run the show, have an agenda, and be ready to adapt as needed. When you can do these things, you will get the most out of meetings you have and your productivity will shine.

CHAPTER 10

Use of Paperwork as an Ultimate Real Estate Investor

One of the things that can strike fear in the heart of the novice investor is the idea of doing paperwork. Perhaps that comes from a lack of familiarity or a fear of fine print, but this issue can be very intimidating and have an influence on how others view you. Your clients will expect that you have some basic understanding of the paperwork you present to them, and the alternative of running everything through an attorney can get expensive real quick. So where does that leave us? I suggest a happy medium, and that medium is the subject of this chapter.

PAPERWORK OVERVIEW

Let's start with a basic overview of what it means to effectively use paperwork in a real estate transaction. Unlike other commodities, real estate can be structured and greatly leveraged when you have a strong command and understanding of the associated paperwork. This is also why paperwork is sometimes intimidating for most people. However intimidating it may seem to you or people you do business with, it is imperative that you strive to fully understand the paperwork you use.

The good news is, getting a thorough knowledge of paperwork can be simplified and learned over time, as we'll discuss here.

As far as simplifying paperwork, my basic suggestion is to create packages of forms for each type of deal you commonly do. This is much easier than needing to scramble around feverishly to gather and print the forms you'll need (while hoping you don't forget something) before you can meet with a new client. The easy way is when you get the phone call, grab the appropriate packet of prepared forms off your shelf and go. Which way seems easier to you? Which way will be less stressful? I think you see my point. Beyond that, let's discuss this further by highlighting the three main kinds of paperwork you'll need.

- Paperwork with sellers (purchase contracts)

- Paperwork with buyers or tenants (sales contracts, leases, etc.)

- Supporting paperwork

Most paperwork fits into one of these three categories, so let's look at each in more detail.

BRIAN'S ULTIMATE RESOURCE

To get a free CD-ROM of the 50 most commonly used real estate investing forms that I personally use in my investing business, go to www.FreeMakeMoneyGift.com.

PURCHASE CONTRACTS

Remember that I don't say the words "purchase contracts" with anyone I do business with. Instead I say, "This is the piece of paper that says you are selling and I am buying." This is less threatening to the other party. For some reason, the word "contract" scares people.

The types of purchase contracts you may wish to use for your deals may vary considerably, and I'm not one to hang my hat on one in particular and suggest it will work well in any situation. First, I'm not in a position to rightfully do so. Second, it just wouldn't be fair for you to be left thinking this is the way to go. Ultimate a contract is just a meeting of the minds between two parties. Every situation is different and your choice of contracts should reflect this. Some basic choices to consider include the following:

- A formal Realtor contract

- A private contract that is full length

- A private contract that is intentionally short

When selecting a purchase contract, remember that beauty is in the eye of the beholder. It's not just about what you prefer to use; it's also a function of what the recipient will think. For example, you may have learned the business from someone who subscribes to the theory that you should use your own paperwork at all times. This is a decent theory, but what happens when you want to pursue listed properties such as a bank-repossessed property? Realtors will often avoid and discourage contracts they are unfamiliar with, so you need to be prepared to use something that is not your own for certain situations.

Although I have conservative political views, I tend to have a more liberal view of contract selection and can easily adapt contracts that aren't from my own library by adding certain key addendums if necessary. Addendums to consider might include a right to show, right to assign, or a right to inspect the property and can include whatever you want to include. This way, any prohibitive features of a foreign contract can be "undone" by the addendums you choose and make the contract more like one you would more normally use. Keep in mind that too many addendums and contingencies in a contract can and will very often kill a deal because it scares the other party away. Keep it simple and only add when necessary.

Some sellers are accustomed to receiving contracts that are of the full-length variety and may object to something that is unusually brief. For simple transactions like cash purchase wholesale (contract assignment) deals, a brief contract is all that is really needed, and you can sell the simplicity to your clients as a reason you are easy to work with. This can add integrity in the right situation. For other, more traditional, deals, even the simple use of addendums or specific terms can show that you are on the top of your game and give you a defined amount of professionalism.

CONTRACTS WITH BUYERS/TENANTS

Paperwork with buyers can be remarkably similar to that for your sellers, so long as you don't forget to remove many of the protective features you might want to see in there as a buyer. You don't want to extend the same flexibility to your buyers unless it is absolutely necessary. Just remember that how you buy and how you sell are not the same. Other types of sales contracts include those used for rental properties or for creatively financed deals like lease options. Examples of such documentation include:

- Residential leases

- Options to purchase

- Land contracts

- Promissory notes

- Mortgage

When you are working with a tenant, a lease form that is approved for your area is advisable, since tenant-landlord rules can vary from place to place. Some tenants are very savvy, and a poorly drafted lease can haunt you later. Creative financing documents come in several forms, and your choice may just be a matter of personal preference.

The key thing to remember is that the paperwork may change, but the basic idea remains the same. A lease option is basically a lease that is accompanied by an option to purchase agreement that gives the occupant an effective first right of refusal to buy the property for a set price. A land contract (also referred to as a contract for deed in some places) is basically a purchase contract that stipulates the completion of the terms between a buyer and seller will result in a transfer of ownership to the buyer. A promissory note is the written promise that one party agrees to repay the other party. A mortgage is the legal instrument that is publically recorded and officially attaches the note to the property as collateral.

I strongly suggest that you always have your attorney close your standard closings and your lease option agreements with your clients. Why, you ask? There are multiple reasons:

1. The fact that you use a professional attorney exhibits a tremendous amount of trustworthiness with the people you do business with.

2. It should cost you nothing, because you are going to have your buyer pay the attorney fee.

3. You have your attorney's blessing when they close your deals.

4. You'll find no better witness if somebody wants to come back and cry foul about something in the agreement down the road.

5. Your chances of people doing what they say they will do are much greater than they would be if you signed closing paperwork with them at a coffee shop. The bottom line is to let the professionals do what they do best so that you can do what you do best.

SUPPORTING PAPERWORK

The paperwork that is more behind the scenes is often just as important as the basic contracts you will use, because they serve two primary functions. First, this type of paperwork helps glue your deals together by answering questions your clients may have and disclosing various other specifics to a deal that your contract might not expand on. Second, this type of paperwork protects you. Whether it's to authorize you to do something pivotal to the completion of the deal or simply what I call a CYA form (covering your assets), sometimes the simplest of forms can go a long way by keeping you from getting into hassles or even legal entanglements with your clients.

EXAMPLES OF SUPPORTING DOCUMENTATION
MIGHT INCLUDE THE FOLLOWING:

- Authorization to release information, allowing you to contact a client's lender

- Affidavits of agreement, allowing you to file the existence of your purchase contract against the title of the property in question, securing your interest in it

- Disclosure forms, good for foreclosures and creative financing deals

- Waiver forms, disclosing what you are and are not responsible for

- Short-sale package documentation

Any of these types of documents are available in many real estate software or contracts packages, and they can be created by a real estate attorney. The more you educate yourself in the business, the more apparent it will be when and where these types of forms need to be used, so pay attention, keep learning, and you'll know better how to use these documents properly.

BRIAN'S KEY POINT

Always have your attorney review your paperwork to make sure that (1) it is your state friendly, and (2) your attorney is comfortable with everything.

I know from experience that your conscience usually wants to trust the other person that you are doing business with in regard to a specific agreement or understanding about something. Unfortunately, when there are two parties involved in a transaction, each party is going to mentally process things differently. And not only that, but when things aren't specifically spelled out and understood in writing, then people automatically assume that they can change their mind about something without consequence. Do they have the right to do this? Perhaps, perhaps not. But the fact of the matter is this, when you do not get things in writing from people you do business with, there is no real consequence or accountability for either party.

Therefore, the solution to this problem is simply always get everything in writing from people you do business with, even when you do business with family or friends. When thoughts are in writing and agreed to up front by all parties, there is a much less chance for future problems and misunderstandings.

This may be considered a commonsense topic, but I would guess that there are a few situations when you wish you had gotten something in writing upfront because it came back to bite you later. There definitely have been for me.

I hope that this chapter has provided you a nice overview of the primary types of paperwork you will be working with as an investor. The general fear is that you will be asked to explain or use a broad scope of contracts and that you will get tripped up in the presence of a client. First of all, when you are working a particular niche in the business, the paperwork you will use is going to be more consistent between various deals than you might think. That should be at least some consolation to you.

My suggestion to help you get past any basic contract-o-phobia is to first sit down and really take a close look at the documents you will be using with your clients. No, you don't have to memorize them line-by-line, and I have yet to work with a client who wanted to go through one line-by-line. That doesn't mean skipping through major sections with no explanation. What it does mean is that you should try and capture the gist of each section and be able to explain in layperson's terms to your clients. This will satisfy most, and if they have issues or questions you can't address or answer, then have them consult with an attorney. This way, you're never on the spot or feel like you need to elaborate on something you don't have the professional qualifications to address.

I would also advise you to sit down with your real estate attorney as you are getting your business going. Have him or her review your paperwork, make suggestions for changes, make them state friendly, and, as needed, help you understand what the content means. This one-time expense can give you a lot more confidence and permit you to announce, when appropriate, that your attorney has reviewed your paperwork. You'll also naturally become more comfortable with your paperwork as time goes on, so that should be of some reassurance. Take this seriously, but also take it easy on yourself. The paperwork dilemma you may be facing right now should work out just fine over time.

CHAPTER 11

Customer Service and Follow-up as an Ultimate Real Estate Investor

Retail businesses are constantly promoting their commitment to customer service and for good reason. Customers are the lifeblood of the business and they must be protected at all costs. You are operating a slightly different kind of business as a real estate investor, but that does not mean customer service is any less important. The ways in which you provide customer service is different, but the general idea remains the same.

The way you service your customers (or clients) as an investor has changed a bit over the years. In old-school real estate investing, investor usually meant landlord, and that was about as popular a role as the local tax collector. Landlords were allowed a lot more flexibility when it came to evictions, problems with tenants, etc. Their form of customer service was to rule with authority, and people respected it or moved on.

The modern investor has to look at the business a little differently. Laws are generally favorable to consumers, and you are one misstep away from being sued in a very litigious society. In short, investors are often asked to tread on eggshells and that has softened the approach many of us take when working with our clients, be they sellers, buyers, or tenants. I'm not suggesting that you need to be soft or shouldn't pursue solutions that are available. What I am saying is that there is more of an expectation that you, as an investor, can better relate to your clients, which can translate to greater profits at reduced risk – if you play your cards right.

DON'T MAKE PROMISES YOU CAN'T KEEP

One of the foremost requirements of being a real estate investor is the consistent interaction with everyday people. To achieve great success, you need to have very confident and personable communication skills. You need to be able to deal with uncomfortable situations. Because the fact of the matter is this: A majority of the people that you do business with are people in distress. Not all, but most.

If you haven't yet, you will eventually find yourself in a situation where you will want to promise the sun the moon and the stars to the person sitting across the table from you. The real estate deal that you are considering will look so sweet and profitable that you'll want to say anything to get the other party to sign paperwork with you.

This is absolutely the wrong approach. The last thing that you ever want to do is find yourself in a situation where you've made a promise to someone and you are uncertain that you'll be able to keep that promise. Here's the reality of the business: Murphy lives everywhere. If something can go wrong, then it probably will. If you have made a promise to someone that you can't keep because of Murphy, then you may find yourself in a very difficult situation. Be honest, and do business with integrity. Don't make false-hope promises or lie to get your way, because then you won't have to remember to whom you lied. Voilà!

INVESTOR-RELATED CUSTOMER SERVICE OFTEN FALLS INTO ONE OF THE FOLLOWING CATEGORIES:

- Relations with sellers

- Negotiating with buyers

- Managing tenants

- Working with team members and other professionals

- Dealing with problems

I will discuss some of the key points you need to keep in mind with each of these categories, and you too will soon see how customer service is more than just a concept but something that spreads throughout your entire business operation.

RELATIONS WITH SELLERS

Sellers are some of the most important clients you'll work with, because they set the table for the rest of your business. They are often uncertain about what you can do for them and may be experiencing highly charged circumstances in their lives. Because of these things, you need to be prepared to guide, educate, encourage, and clarify all with the same client. Sellers want to work with you, so don't give them a reason to think otherwise.

The key with sellers is that those who are highly motivated may be placing a lot of stock in what you can do for them. They will be paying close attention to what you are doing and you need to set a good example. For example, call back when you say you will, be at meetings on time, and be ready to take charge of your meetings, as these will all be expectations from your client. None of this falls into the above and beyond the call of duty category, but too many investors fall short of the basics and end up disenchanting a client who was otherwise ready to go.

Remember, too, that a client will often be seeking guidance from you, and it is not at all improper to give them a list of things they need to do on their own behalf. For example, you may suggest that they assemble financial information, lender documentation, etc. You will be reasonable in asking a seller to provide these, and if you are doing your part to stay on top of customer service, they are much more likely to cooperate.

The best thing you can do when working with sellers is to be personable and professional and try to gain some perspective by putting yourself in their position. (Remember empathy?) Think about what they might be going through and what you would be thinking if you were them. This alone can help craft how you approach a particular seller and the effort, however silent, will give you huge respect. It shows the client that you are able to really identify with their situations.

NEGOTIATING WITH BUYERS

So you have a property ready for sale, and you can already count the dollars that will be going into your bank account when all is said and done. It's an exciting time and one of the many things that keeps investors inspired. It can also be a challenging time and one that can put you at risk, especially when you are new to the business. Why, you ask? It's because you run the risk here of becoming motivated yourself, and that can lead to impulsive or hasty decisions that can cost your business if you aren't careful.

There are some simple ways to manage the sales process that will help keep your business and profits in line with where they should be. First, consider using a Realtor if you have a good one and would rather not tackle this yourself. I don't recommend this for all situations, but it can be an effective route to at least consider. If you're going to handle the sale yourself, there are things you'll want to keep in mind that will help reduce your stress level and maximize your profits.

If you are brave enough, avoid showing your houses; however, if you must show them yourself, try to focus on group showings or open houses, which can save huge amounts of time, show that you are in charge, and also create friendly competition among buying prospects. If you get into the habit of showing to individuals, it can consume your time quickly, leaving less of you to go around. Make sure serious buyers are willing to leave a small deposit to secure their place in line and handle it like you're in charge of every step, and you'll have the most success here.

When it comes time to seal the deal, and involve the buyer with paperwork, remember that you don't have to sell to them. Rather, you simply want to stay in charge of the contracts and paperwork. There's no reason to give up control of this critical part of the process, and when you stay in command of the flow of the deal, your professionalism and customer service both will be respected. Buyers (whether they admit it or not) like working with someone who is aware and in charge of the process more than someone who simply gives them what they think they want.

MANAGING TENANTS

It is no great revelation that working with tenants can be one of the more frustrating aspects of any real estate business. Tenants have their own agenda, sometimes see value in skipping payments or annoying their landlords with all kinds of complaints or requests, and certainly tenants don't see things from a business perspective as you do. This can be challenging to deal with at times and is the primary reason many landlords choose to use professional property management companies to handle this for them. I certainly recommend it, but I know that many of you will be managing some or all of your properties, so a few customer service tips in this area will be helpful.

The most fundamental thing to remember when working with tenants is that you are not operating on their schedule. If I had a dollar for every time a tenant called with an "emergency" that ended up being a little more than a nuisance, I'd have a pretty big piggy bank full of dollars. The fact remains that how you respond to tenant issues can set the tone for what lies ahead. If you are immediately responsive and bend over backward to accommodate a tenant, they will soon expect it every time and can make your life miserable. I'm not saying to go to the opposite extreme and ignore things, but just be careful here because they aren't necessarily your friends and they won't pay you any more rent just because you're eager to take care of issues they bring to your attention.

The best landlords I've seen are pleasant and cordial, but swing a big stick when they need to. They handle problems that arise when they are able to get to them and don't accept excuses or niceness from a tenant as reasons to cut them any slack. When you can take a similar approach to customer service with your own tenants, your role as a landlord will be much easier and better respected.

WORKING WITH TEAM MEMBERS AND OTHER PROFESSIONALS

How you interact with team members or other business professionals is really where you have a chance to shine. More so than with your regular clients, you may be dealing with team members more often, so how you approach customer service and time management will be often more apparent to them than to a client who is selling a property. Some of the basic essentials ring true for any type of customer service, but there are also some elements that are more unique to this type of client relationship.

Common threads include prompt returns of phone calls or e-mails, showing up on time for scheduled meetings, and effective follow-up when it comes to checking on progress a particular team member should be making for one or more of your deals. These elements are just good business, and you should expect it of yourself as much as your clients will expect it from you.

BRIAN'S JOURNAL ENTRY

"My Biggest Pet Peeve on the Planet"

You may find that this little section is less a personal story and more of a time for me to vent.

We all have pet peeves, the things that annoy us that other people do or don't do, and it seems like the older I get the longer my list of pet peeves grows. Although I don't actually keep track of my pet peeves on a regular basis, I can't help but note more and more encounters with people and businesses (large and small) that don't do what they say.

As an entrepreneur and business owner, I pride myself and my staff on doing what we say and going above and beyond the call of duty to see things through. Very rarely do I give people and businesses a second chance once they have defaulted on their commitments. It is as simple as this: If you say you are going to do something, then do it. If you are at all unsure that you will do something, then don't do it. It's about doing business with simple courtesy and personal accountability, and it starts with keeping your commitments about returning a phone call when you say you'll return it, or meeting someone for lunch at the agreed upon time. A majority of this world has lost touch with personal accountability and responsibility.

I am sharing my venting with you because I want to you be mega successful as a real estate investor. If this is something that you need to fix, then do it quickly; otherwise, word will spread and your image can become quickly tarnished. The super-successful entrepreneurs of this world will all agree with me. If you want to get to the top, then you must pride yourself on doing what you say you'll do. This habit will reflect in your relationships and overall respect that you will receive from the people you do business with.

What makes interacting with team members a little different is that the same customer service elements that apply to you should also apply to them. You should expect that they return phone calls or e-mails promptly. You should expect that they be on time for meetings and be prepared for them when you arrive. You should expect that they follow up with you if they need something. This is also good customer service on their part and you have every right to expect that of them. After all, they are also professional businesspeople and their business, just like yours, also has reliance upon good customer service.

BRIAN'S KEY POINT

Only do business with people who want to do business with you. Manage your relationships with this attitude and things will be much simpler.

When this aspect falls short (or at least does so too often), you have the prerogative to change whom you use and sometimes they need to know that. You don't want to have a quick trigger with team members, but you also shouldn't settle for poor service, as your ability to do business can be affected (your time, money, and reputation) by how well they perform.

DEALING WITH PROBLEMS

Recall what I said earlier that Murphy lives everywhere. Unfortunately, things do not always go as planned, and problems arise when you least expect. The most important thing you can do when problems arise is, first, to identify the root of the problem. Second, be proactive to solve the problem. The longer you let the problem fester, the worse the problem gets and the more it keeps you awake at night. If you are unsure how to solve the problem in a particular situation, then get advice from someone who does. No, I'm not referring to your brother. I'm referring to your attorney. Sure, you'll have to pay for this advice but, depending on the problem, it could be cheap insurance to avoid a bigger financial hit down the road.

Remember when I alluded to the retail concept of customer service at the beginning of the chapter? The mantra here is usually a reference to the customer always being right or that you should otherwise bend over backward to accommodate the customer. In real estate, my version of customer service is a little different. I want to be pleasant and congenial, but also exhibit a level of professional authority when necessary.

The customer-is-always-right approach to managing tenants is a recipe for disaster, as is going the extra mile to make a seller happy with your asking price. You can be accommodating, but still must operate according to the principles that will make you successful as a real estate investor. Perhaps the best way to achieve this happy medium is to be armed and ready with other concessions that can be offered in lieu of giving up something more fundamental like price or monthly rent.

Another way to look at the customer service game in real estate is that you aren't usually dealing with a lot of repeat customers. That's not to say you should take a rigid stance because of this, but look at the facts. If you have a property for sale, you want the ideal buyer, and if you're marketing it properly, you should have plenty of interest. Why bend over backward to accommodate one client as if he or she were your only viable buying prospect? Treat every client equally in terms of how you approach them, but you can only sell to one and must make the decision that is best for your business.

When every one of your clients feels like they are important to you, the mission of customer service as an investor is accomplished. Even if you don't buy a property from Client X or sell a property to Client Y, their experience in working with you should be positively memorable. That gives you a level of professional authority that is unmistakable, especially since your competition will not likely be doing the same thing.

BRIAN'S ULTIMATE RESOURCE

I created a free four-CD-ROM and manual course for you, which I will deliver to your door (while supplies last) for the mere cost of shipping and handling. It's called "The 77 Biggest Mistakes Real Estate Investors Make."

It is an incredible follow-up to this book and outlines the 77 biggest business-killing and costly real estate investing mistakes, all of which I have personally faced being in this business, and details how I overcame them. To get your free course, go to

www.FreeMakeMoneyGift.com.

CHAPTER 12

Understanding Your Role With the IRS and Basic Asset Protection

Disclosure: Information within is not to be considered as legal, tax, or financial advice. You should check with your lawyer, accountant, and professional financial advisor before acting on this or any information.

Demonstrating and honing your skills and professional expertise is vital to your success when working with clients and peers. It is equally as important to maintain credibility with Uncle Sam. After all, taxes are an inevitable part of running a business, and while they can be effectively reduced in many ways, they also need to be accounted for. The way in which your business is set up can have a big impact on how you are viewed, tax-wise, and thus directly and indirectly influence your professional longevity.

Basically, it works like this. When you decide you're going to go into business as a real estate investor, there are a number of ways in which you can do it. The easiest way is to simply leave things as they are, operating as an individual and simply enjoying some tax breaks for the properties you are able to accumulate. That said, there are some significant disadvantages of this approach, even if it is the easiest way to go.

First, you lose out on some substantial tax deductions when you operate your business as an individual. Expenses that are at least partially deductible for businesses are generally not deductible for you if you are not operating as an organized business, for example:

- Marketing expenses

- Utilities pertinent to your business operation

- Phone and Internet

- Vehicle expenses/mileage

- Supplies

- Meals or entertainment with clients

Your team accountant has the final word when it comes to deductions, but these kinds of expenses are typically (1) available to businesses and (2) not available to individuals, so consider this lack of business structure carefully if you are thinking about it, because it can greatly affect your bank account.

Another clear disadvantage of not using a business structure relates to liability. Business entities allow properties you own as investments to be titled in a name other than your own. Many states have homestead laws that allow liability protection for one's personal residence, but these rules usually don't apply to investment properties, so you need to be careful. You are investing in assets that ideally have tangible value that can make you an attractive target if your business operations don't do much to protect the assets you accumulate.

Since there are some clear advantages to protecting your business assets, as well as enjoying additional tax breaks, what options do you have for organizing your business? There are several ways, and you should decide which is best for you with the help of your team accountant and/or real estate attorney, as this is their place to shine. Let the professionals do what they do best.

As I suggested, there are several options for business organization. These are:

- Sole proprietorship
- Corporation
- Limited liability company (LLC)
- Limited partnership

I will briefly discuss each of these entities below; however, my best advice to you is don't go forming any entities until you know why you should be forming them. If you have yet to do a single deal, then why do you need a business entity? Go make a big fat check and then consult with someone to get your business set up properly. Although having an entity is important, it is not required to start doing deals.

Some entities are better suited for different business applications than others. I will follow that discussion with a few other helpful tax-saving tips that can be well worth the effort as an investor and businessperson.

SOLE PROPRIETORSHIP

A sole proprietorship is basically a business that is run by a person and operates under that person's social security number. There is no separate entity formed. The advantage of a sole proprietorship is that a person who files taxes in this way can start claiming the tax benefits of being in business without having to file for a corporation or LLC. A sole proprietor's business identity is usually a "doing business as" (DBA) kind of arrangement and is less organized than a formal business entity.

As I mentioned before, the tax advantages of being a sole proprietor are not that different from other kinds of business structures. There are two key differences that you should be aware of, though. First, sole proprietorships open you up to personal liability for the activities of the business, putting your assets at greater risk. Second, the IRS is far more likely to audit you (or at least pay extra close attention to your business tax deductions) when you are a sole proprietor than a separate business entity. For many investors who don't yet have assets that they have acquired, a sole proprietorship is something to at least consider.

CORPORATION

A corporation is one of the easiest and most effective ways to give your business a more defined identity and also allow it to enjoy some of the more tangible benefits of being in business. Corporations (and LLCs, too, for that matter) are fairly easy to establish and also easy to maintain. Most states allow corporations to be filed online and the set-up process is easier than you might think. Basically, wanting to start a business is all that is necessary to form a corporation. There's no application process, approval needed, or minimum amount of capital to do this.

Once you form a corporation, you can then set up a bank account in the name of the corporation and start routing expenses and revenue through it. This allows you to more effectively separate your business actions from your personal affairs, which is an important distinction when it comes to taxes and the IRS. Expenses run through a corporate account are generally much easier to claim as tax deductible, even though this is not an excuse to manage company funds improperly.

Unlike LLCs or limited partnerships, corporations are generally not the best entities in which to hold assets, and many asset protection specialists would recommend a corporation for business operations and one or more alternate entities that would house the assets (in your case, real estate). Basically, like other formal business entities, corporations make it easier to account for company expenses and are also less prone to extra scrutiny by the IRS. Given their relatively low expense to establish, they are worthy of serious consideration.

LIMITED LIABILITY COMPANY (LLC)

The limited liability company (or LLC) is a fairly new kind of business entity, but has been around long enough to be battle-tested in legal settings. LLCs have some advantages other entities do not. LLCs are fundamentally partnerships, so they have members, rather than officers and directors like a corporation. They can be set up to emulate the tax benefits of corporations but also can be effective entities in which to hold real estate assets. LLCs are seen as generally being much better for asset protection than corporations, even if the tax advantages between the two are probably a draw.

Operating an LLC gives you a similar level of identity and authority to that of a corporation. Clients will note that you have a company and can even look you up in some states to verify that your company actually exists and is registered in the state. Like corporations, don't overdo your stated title within your company. What you do is far more influential than what your official title is. Remember, you are working on Main Street, not Wall Street.

LIMITED PARTNERSHIP

Limited partnerships are common business structures for larger projects, as they are ideal for situations where moneys need to be raised to fund a deal. Basically, a limited partnership works like this. A general partner manages the partnership, carries a small percentage of the ownership and a high percentage of the liability. Numerous limited partners carry the majority of the ownership but have almost no liability. In this way, actions brought against the limited partnership (such as a lawsuit) end up in the hands of the general partner, who owns next to nothing, as far as the total partnership value.

Limited partnerships are great tools to raise money and protect the interests of the contributors. They aren't necessarily of much general use to the average real estate investor who buys houses here and there. Typically, these structures are more suited for land projects or commercial real estate and may be worth exploring based on your individual needs.

LAND TRUST

Land trusts are one of the most popular vehicles in which to take title to investment and personal real estate. Ask any experienced real estate investor and he probably has used this vehicle or has heard of its benefits. The main reason for using this vehicle is privacy and separation of assets. The land trust, however, does not provide asset protection. I highly recommend you use a land trust in conjunction with an LLC or other asset-protection entity.

To combat the challenges to real estate ownership, many experienced real estate investors have turned to a land trust to find solace. A land trust is a revocable grantor trust; hence, it is protected under the Garn St. Germain Depository Institutions Act of 1982. In fact, the land trust is very similar to a living trust, but only slightly modified to achieve different results.

A LAND TRUST, LIKE A LIVING TRUST, HAS FOUR COMPONENTS:

1. Grantor: The person who establishes the trust

2. Trustee: The person or entity that holds the trust property for the benefit of the trust beneficiaries. The trustee holds title for the benefit of the grantor (in this case, the grantor is also the beneficiary). If you place a title to your property in a land trust, you have not violated the due-on-sale (if occupancy does not change).

3. Beneficiary: The person or entity that receives the benefit of the trust property

4. Trust assets: The property that is deeded into the name of the trust

The experienced investor who wishes to grow a quiet empire will do so with the help of a land trust. Do you want every person with a computer finding out how many properties you own and what you are worth with a few simple keystrokes? Think about it. Owning real estate in your own name is like walking around passing out your financial statement to everyone you meet. In the United States, copies of real estate deeds are recorded for the public to view at their convenience. When done right, your investments can be held on public record but in private.

THERE ARE TWO PAPER PARTS TO A LAND TRUST:

1. Warranty deed to trustee, which gets recorded and puts the property in a land trust.

2. Agreement and declaration of trust, which shows beneficial interest and is *not* recorded. (This document is private and no one can get a copy of it unless you give it to him or her or they have a court order.)

LAND TRUST MIND MAP 1

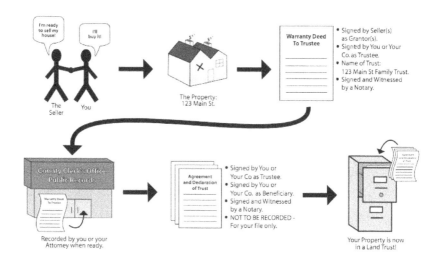

LAND TRUST MIND MAP 2

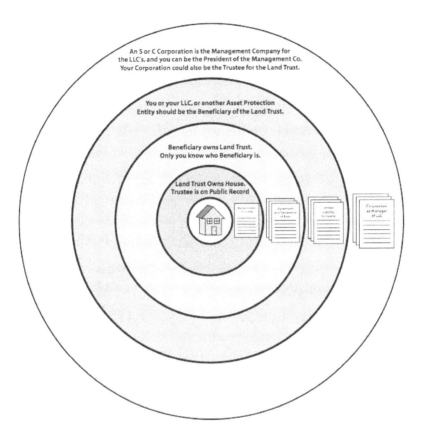

ADDITIONAL TIPS/COMMENTS ON LAND TRUSTS

- The trustee can be any person or entity of your choosing (someone you trust).

- It doesn't matter where the trustee lives.

- You don't need anyone's permission to use a land trust.

- Each house should be in its own land trust (do not combine).

- There is no federal ID reporting or special accounting required for a land trust.

- You can always take property out of a land trust at anytime.

- Land trusts works in every state.

- It is a nontaxable entity.

- Once a property is deeded out of a land trust, the trust is dead.

- Name your land trust: 123 Main St. Family Trust or The Jones Family Trust

- The trustee is not liable for any actions of the trust.

- The trustee does nothing but sign the deed at purchase and sale of the property.

- A land trust does not have an associated bank account.

- List the trust as an additional insured on your insurance policy.

- The IRS doesn't care who the beneficial interest of the trust is. All the IRS cares about is the money coming in and out of the property and what entity you are reporting it in.

- The beneficial interest and trustee should be different entities/people.

- Your LLC or an asset-protection entity should be the beneficiary of the trust.

TAX-SAVING TIPS

In addition to simply forming a business entity, there are some other useful vehicles for saving on taxes. This is not a discussion of business write-offs, but of techniques and tips for keeping more of your revenue, such as:

- 1031 tax exchanges

- Use of living trusts

- Dividend-paying whole-life insurance

- Retirement accounts

- Self-directed IRA

In the case of exchanges and trusts, these tools allow for transfers or upgrades of assets without being subject to substantial capital gains taxes. Sure, there are rules and regulations for how to do this properly, but that is a better question for an accountant or estate attorney.

In the case of whole-life insurance or retirement accounts, these tools allow you to use capital housed in them to invest in real estate or other commodities. The return that is paid back to them can be structured to where it is tax-deferred or, in some cases, even tax-free. Ask your team members about these kinds of tools for your business, and also keep your eyes peeled at your local REIA meetings, because these also are common discussion topics.

Winning the game of business and tax savings is not about beating or outsmarting the IRS. That is old-school thinking. If you have to write a big ugly check to Uncle Sam, then this means that you had a decent year. Go make more money and hope that you'll have to write a bigger check next year.

BRIAN'S KEY POINT

Remember, your duty as a business owner and real estate investor is to focus on revenue, not cost control.

Many of us have the mindset that sticking it to the taxman is good, which implies an adversarial relationship with the government's tax system. That just isn't the case when it comes to running a business. Without a doubt, the best way to minimize your taxes is to be a business owner. Companies are taxed in a lower bracket than individual earners and, to boot, are taxed on net income, not gross income like everyone else. That itself is a huge plus for bringing more organization to your business.

When it comes to how you are viewed in the eyes of the IRS, the exact stats are staggering. Corporations and LLCs that claim certain business deductions are some 7 to 10 times less likely to be audited than a sole proprietor who makes the same deduction claims. Why? A corporation is a business that usually has its own tax identity and thus is less likely to throw up red flags to auditors. Individuals have every right to run their own businesses without the use of an entity, but they also must be more cautious when it comes to deducting expenses. The IRS simply keeps a closer eye on sole proprietorships, due to past and present abuse of the business deductions that are allowed. Whatever you do, keep good financial records and you'll have little to worry about.

One more secret tip when it comes to taxes. Come tax time each April 15th, I have my CPA file an extension for me whether or not I need it. I do this for two primary reasons: (1) I don't want my CPA to rush through my taxes during this very busy time of year, and (2) I am strategically trying to minimize my chances for a tax audit. Ninety percent of all taxpayers file their return before the April 15th deadline, and if you've learned anything from reading this book, it should be that I don't do or teach how to do things like everyone else. During the time the IRS will be doing all its audits for the current tax year, I will just be filing my return. I don't do this because I am attempting to hide anthying, but rather I am merely trying to minimize my chances for an unnecessary audit. This was advice given to me years ago by a multimillionaire, and now I am sharing this information with you.

In summary, when the government makes it clear that incorporating or registering an LLC is a proven way to reduce your risk of tax audits, why not go with it? These entities can also be better ways to protect assets, and once you have assets worth protecting, you can and should want to do everything you can to protect them from financial predators.

CHAPTER 13

Working With Private Lenders as an Ultimate Real Estate Investor

Majority of this book is about how to make money in real estate without money, and as I have discussed there are countless ways to do this. That being said, there are times when access to money (not yours) can help you multiply your profits, ease the tension of closings, and assist with cash flow. This is where private money comes in.

You might have the best business plan in the world and all the drive to be successful that a person can have, but there are always limits to what you can do with your own resources. We've all been there. You start out, pick up a property or two here and there, market like you should, and at some point you hit a wall. The well of capital runs dry and that leaves you with some serious decisions to make. This concept of "What now?" is not often addressed in real estate books or seminars and leaves many investors frustrated when they reach this point in their business. So, what do you do?

The idea of raising business capital is the answer to this dilemma and there are several ways to do it. One is to work with either local or national lenders to establish business lines of credit. Some of these are very simple and require no more than a business entity and decent personal credit. Others may require asset verification and can become larger and larger over time. A second option is to attract and raise private money.

Private money has been a foundational element of new businesses for a long time. What do you think fueled the dot-com boom in the late 1990s? Much of the capital that poured into the tech industry during this time period was private money and a lot of people and businesses got wealthy as a result. It is not at all uncommon for a business to seek and raise capital to support its growth and development, so why should your business be any different? When investing correctly, I believe that you can offer private lenders a much safer return than any stock in the stock market.

If you feel there is a need in your business to use money for various real estate deals, then this is a topic you need to pay close attention to. Since many investors attract capital from individuals who are not formally licensed to loan money, the term that is often used in real estate is a "private mortgage lender." This chapter will explore some of the intricacies of raising funds like this for your own business.

FINDING PRIVATE MORTGAGE LENDERS

One of the greatest things about using private lenders is that they can come from almost anywhere. They can be friends, family, or Joe Blow down the street. They could be conspicuous high earners, like doctors or lawyers, or the millionaire farmer who still drives the ratty old pickup truck everywhere he goes. They could be obvious (like your professional team members) or completely unexpected, like someone you're sitting next to on a plane. You just never know, and you need to be prepared for whatever circumstances come your way.

The critical first step in finding private mortgage lenders is to start acting like a businessperson who is looking for venture capital. Chances are a private lender is not going to come up to you one day to ask if you need money. I'm sure that has happened in the course of investing history, but it is not common and you shouldn't expect it to work like that. Your microphone should be on at all times, and you should be networking your business regularly. Be ready to promote what you do and talk the business of private mortgage loans when the topic does come up.

As you might expect, a big part of your success with private mortgage lenders will be your perceived credibility. You've probably heard of the term "credibility kit" before. A basic credibility kit for the real estate investor has a number of advantages, including:

- Being able to present a basic summary of your business to others

- Being a foundation for your marketing program

- Offering an organized business summary to bankers, private lenders, and other team members

All of these advantages are equally important. I believe it is important to briefly discuss some of the primary components of a credibility kit, so you can begin to assemble yours as soon as possible. There is no universally recognized template for such a kit, but the following list will give you a good idea of how to get started. A good credibility kit includes:

- A nice cover letter that introduces you and your business

- A summary of your business philosophy, focus areas, and experience

- Examples of how you market your business

- Deals you have completed (if applicable)

- An excerpt or full copy of a business plan

- Testimonial letters and recommendation letters

These components together paint the picture that your business is for real, has focus and direction, and is well organized. All of these convey serious credibility and this is why the credibility kit is such a useful tool for your business. Not only will your own kit make you accountable to its contents and help you focus your efforts as your business grows in success, it will also give you a tremendous amount of confidence.

This type of kit is perhaps most useful because private lending prospects will likely want to see something about you before offering their funds. When you have something to offer them that describes who you are, what you do, and a little about your business vision, you're well on your way. Once you can engage a prospect in the subject of money, you need to know what terms are to be agreed upon, and that is my next subject for discussion.

SECURING FUNDS FROM PRIVATE LENDERS

Once you have your foot in the door, you need to be ready to seal the deal with a prospective private lender. It is important that you capture their interest first – before ever putting a live deal in front of them – for two key reasons. First, you want them to see value in your business, not just a single deal, since this lends itself (no pun intended) to future deals beyond the first one. Second (and perhaps more important), capturing their interest before putting their funds in a specific deal keeps you in better compliance with securities laws.

I know I just popped open a can of worms there, didn't I? Securities law? Before you get nervous, let me give you the quick highlights. When you capture interest from a private lender, they're only seeing value in a business model before committing any funds. They aren't being presented with a specific opportunity until after they've agreed to provide some funding for your business. This means they haven't been formally solicited for funding, which is more closely governed by the laws that concern investments. Just stay away from randomly soliciting funds for a specific deal and you should be OK. I, of course, may be missing a detail or two, so be sure to run all this by your attorney to make sure you are doing everything correctly.

Now I that have covered the bases, I will now discuss what you need to agree on with your lenders. Example terms for an agreement with a private lender include:

- The length of the loan

- The amount that is being borrowed

- The return that is expected

HOW TO MAKE MONEY IN YOUR LOCAL REAL ESTATE MARKET

- The means by which the loan will be repaid (usually a fixed return rate or sometimes profit sharing)

- Recourse if the loan is not paid back on time

There may be some other case-by-case terms, but these are the main things you need to work out with a private lender. Ways to put all this to paper can vary and I highly suggest you work with your attorney to get it all put together because your lenders will probably be having their attorney review it as well.

MANAGING RELATIONSHIPS WITH PRIVATE LENDERS

Like any situation where there is a capital investment, private lenders are going to have certain expectations of you as the source of their eventual returns. The first and best thing you can do is to structure your agreements correctly the first time around. What I mean here is that the majority of challenges that arise with private lending relationships rely too much on a best-case scenario and too little of the real world. This can apply to both the repayment terms and also the timing, and is easy to avoid.

I need to elaborate just a little on what I mentioned in the previous paragraph. Many private lending relationships can proceed without incident and this is, of course, the idea. When problems do arise, they are usually because the borrower needs more money or because he or she needs more time in which to pay the lender back. These situations, when they do occur, are often because the borrower is trying too hard to accommodate a lender and suggests they "probably" only need so much capital or "should" be able to get a project done in so much time. It's easy to see how this can happen and hopefully also why you want to avoid this.

My simple suggestions here are twofold. First, ask for more funding than you think you'll need. If this means padding your budget a little bit, so be it. Extra expenses do come up with real estate projects and sometimes (in fact, all too often) they take longer than originally anticipated, increasing the necessary carrying costs. It's always easier to ask for the extra funding up front, because the alternatives are either go back to the lender and ask for more money or to come up with it yourself. Neither situation is ideal. Asking for more money from a private lender on the same deal could prove to be damaging to your relationship.

Timing is another issue to approach with caution when it comes to private lenders. Many will like the idea of getting a quick turnaround on their investment and may actually push for these short time frames (e.g., six months or less). It is tempting to go for this as an investor, thinking that a short time frame should work out OK. My suggestion is to stop right there and reconsider before going any further. Just like running out of money, having to approach your lenders to say you need more time could be a relationship killer.

Now let's say, for the sake of an example, that the worst did happen and you needed more time to pay back the lender. Put yourself in the private lender's shoes to determine how you would like to be treated. Consider drafting a formal business letter explaining the situation and respectfully requesting a restructure of the original note. I've had to do this before with one of my private lenders and it was surprisingly well-received. I am now viewed with more professionalism and a greater sense of credibility because I was proactive and sought out a solution with plenty of time to spare on our original note agreement.

The solution here is simple. Anticipate as best you can the realistic time frame you think will be necessary for your deal, and then double it. The likely worst-case scenario is that your project is completed (at least from your private lender's point of view) on time, whereas the best-case scenario is that you'll finish before a deadline.

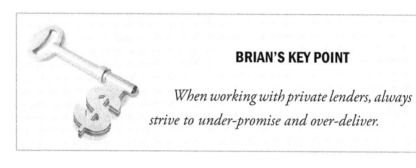

BRIAN'S KEY POINT

When working with private lenders, always strive to under-promise and over-deliver.

The bottom line is to look at what you are offering from the lender's perspective. What would you be looking for if you were going to lend money to a real estate investor? What security instruments would you want to see in place? What assurances on time would you find appropriate? How would you want him or her to handle challenges along the way? What would make you want to do it all over again? When you think like this, your pursuit of private lending will be much more productive, profitable, and repetitive.

The idea of using private lenders is nothing new in the world of real estate investing. Successful investors have been raising and using private capital for decades and it is only now starting to filter down to the novice investor as being something of great importance. Does this mean that it should be something you look at carefully? Absolutely. How fast do you want your business to grow? There's the slow route and the progressive fast track, and private lending can quickly put you on the fast track to success.

Like any business decision, the choice to pursue private lenders comes with its upsides and downsides. The upsides are pretty clear, as there is a virtually limitless supply of capital that is out there. The downsides are few, but the use of private capital does usually require that your business be a little more organized to have the most success raising funds. For example, your credibility kit and business plan are of high importance to a potential private lender even if they might not be as important to other clients.

BRIAN'S ULTIMATE RESOURCE

If you would like to have my "Everything You Need To Attract Private Lenders" kit, with all the forms, reports, commitment letters, and more that I use in my personal real estate investing business, then go to www.FreeMakeMoneyGift.com.

As far as managing the funding you do secure, be bold but also be smart. When making offers, consider that the quality of the deal doesn't just affect you. When you are setting a budget for the deal, it is good practice to imagine yourself in the shoes of the private lender who is funding your deal. I find that when you look at private money as if it were your own, your decisions remain on a better plane and you are less likely to take unnecessary risks. People get funny about money sometimes, but don't let that in any way discourage you. This is a wonderful resource to pursue, and when you pursue it intelligently, the sky's the limit.

CHAPTER 14

Conclusion

Congratulations, you've reached the end of this book – and the beginning of so many exciting and new things for you. By now, you should have a better understanding of what it takes to create a solid and reputable foundation for your business in your local market. It's important to recognize and embrace the topics discussed within this book and the effect they can have on the overall success and longevity of your business. Ultimately, your commitment (or lack thereof) to your real estate education will shape just about everything that has to do with the success you achieve as a real estate investor. I hope this book has helped you to see more clearly the elements and traits needed for you become an ultimate real estate investor.

Normally, this is the point at which I give you that last little bit of motivation to go out there and make it happen. You'll often hear references to corporate slogans or clichés that drive this point home, and as much as I think that is important, I prefer to do things a little differently. After all, this entire book has been about helping you to discover how to establish an outrageously successful real estate investing business in your area. After completing this book, do not simply let up and forget to implement the business-altering information you have now taken in. You need to keep the momentum going and continue to pursue all things that will make you more skilled, more successful, and more wealthy as a result.

A significant part of your success immediately following the moment when you read the last page and put this book down will hinge on your ability to fill in the gaps in your business. I'm convinced that many of you are doing or have done some or even many of the things I have described. If so, great! You're on your way, but the job isn't done just yet. You need to make sure you are doing all of the things I've talked about, because it takes only one negative instance for a client or peer to find you less credible – and that credibility may be hard to rebuild. For now, let's look at a suggested plan of action that follows the outline of the book.

60-DAY PLAN OF ACTION

- Take some time and write down 10 to 20 short-term and long-term goals. Good goals have three key elements. They are (1) specific, (2) written, and (3) in the present tense. For the last part, think of goals if they were happening today. For example, a properly written goal could be, "It is December 1, 2012. I have 10 cash-flowing rental properties in my real estate portfolio."

- Use your long-term goals to create action lists for each week. For example, if you stated a goal to have 20 deals secured in 12 months, how many clients will you have to contact (and then make offers to) to secure those 20? How many clients will you need to speak to on a weekly basis?

- Determine what marketing materials you will use first to get your phone to ring. Refer back to Chapter 1.

- Think carefully about what niche in real estate you would really like to focus on. When you select a niche that is profitable and also enjoyable to you, your passion for the business will grow and it will show to your clients. Refer back to Chapter 5.

- Interview the prospective team members currently missing from your team. The most important of these, from a business-growth standpoint, are a real estate attorney, a CPA, a title company, a mortgage broker, and a real estate agent/ broker. Refer back to Chapter 2.

- If you have a team assembled, meet with your current team members and discuss what you're planning. The more familiar they are with your business objectives, the better they will be able to serve your needs. Refer back to Chapter 9.

- Create a list of at least 20 people who may be good prospective private lenders. Avoid the thinking that anyone would be a poor choice. You don't know if you don't approach them. Refer back to Chapter 13.

- Evaluate your current marketing plan and create or purchase any pieces that are missing. Refer back to Chapter 1.

- Use the information provided to start assembling a credibility kit that can be presented to your clients. Refer back to Chapter 13.

- Reread this book as needed to refresh the topics of interest.

- Consider forming a corporation or LLC if you haven't already done so. Check with a real estate attorney about which is best for you in your particular state. Refer back to Chapter 12.

- Begin working on an organized business plan, using the tips and suggestions I have provided.

- Put together some financial projections that can become a part of your business plan.

- Join a real estate investors' club if you haven't already done so. Attend at least one meeting to start networking with other investors. There is potential here for great networking and in filling any holes in your team.

- Expand your marketing, pick a niche on which you want to focus, and make lots of offers. It's a simple process. Follow your own criteria for evaluating deals. If the numbers don't work, move on to the next one. Refer back to Chapter 9.

- Learn the paperwork that you will use with all of your clients. While your real estate attorney may prepare some documents, it is also important to be versed on what documents are used, when they should be used, and for what purpose. Refer back to Chapter 10.

Once you have an action plan, and I highly recommend that you make the effort to create your own for your business as it grows and develops, the most important next step is to follow it. Action plans may look great sitting next to your desk, but remember that your office is not a common place where you will be looking to invite and impress clients, especially if it's a home office. Your action plan is for you! It should help maintain your focus, motivate you, and remind you of the things that are critical to the success of your business. Now, it's time to get it done.

TROUBLESHOOTING YOUR BUSINESS

I want to briefly discuss the idea of troubleshooting your business, as it is something that I haven't gone into in any great detail previously. Sometimes a conversation, meeting, or even a potential deal will encounter some snags and put your professionalism on the line. This can be an unnerving experience, especially if you're new to the business, so I want to give you a couple of quick suggestions that will help if and when this does happen to you.

First, think about this from the big picture. Remember, "You have to break some eggs to make an omelet," and that concept applies here. You're going to make some mistakes. Whether it's saying the wrong thing at the wrong time, making a wrong decision, or not being prepared for a particular situation, it's going to happen and we've all been there. The key is to not make the same mistakes over and over again. One time is a learning experience. More than once, well, then the idea is not sinking in. Repeated mistakes are the most damaging to your business, because they establish a pattern of bad habits.

BRIAN'S KEY POINT

When things go wrong (and they will), correct the problem as quickly as possible, learn from it, and move on immediately

Second, have high integrity when dealing with all people. This is a people business, and people can be quite forgiving if you make the effort to correct a mistake that you made. In fact, righting a wrong can be respected and a positive trait, because it shows you care about your clients and are willing to go the extra mile when need be. The best way to gauge this issue is to simply ask yourself what you'd like to see done if you were in the client's position. Be smart about it, but when you are committed to a favorable outcome and can correct things that can and will go wrong, it says a lot about you and how you run your business.

TWELVE REASONS MOST REAL ESTATE INVESTORS DON'T REACH THEIR FULL POTENTIAL

In all my years as a real estate investor, I have discovered the 12 reasons why most real estate investors don't reach their full potential:

1. They fear the unknown.

2. They do the wrong things and get lousy results.

3. They procrastinate.

4. They can't prioritize their time.

5. They don't know what to do first or thereafter.

6. They still believe they must have money or credit to succeed.

7. They listen to dream-stealers.

8. They have too many past failures to make room for future successes.

9. They are afraid they won't be able to sell the house after they buy it.

10. They have already spent a lot of money on unsuccessful training programs.

11. They just can't stay focused and organized long enough to maintain forward progress.

12. They don't get their phone to ring consistently with new deals.

I know from personal experience that real estate investing is a tough business, and it can seem like a tremendous battle in the very beginning. I also know from personal experience that it is easy to go flat sometimes.

BRIAN'S ULTIMATE RESOURCE

So what now? Well, if you are a victim of any one of the above 12 reasons, then just know that you are not alone and that you have found the right place to finally help you succeed. As an Ultimate Real Estate Investor I will mail you a 20-plus-page newsletter that I personally write, and a 60-minute CD to keep you motivated and current with all my "what's working today strategies." In addition, you'll be able to participate in a weekly private-line conference call, get deal assistance from me and my staff, a members-only resources Web site, and so much more!

Go to www.UltimateRealEstateInvestors.com and sign up to become a VIP member today. You'll get an incredible free gift and a free trial to test me out!

NEVER GIVE UP

I know that the phrase "Never give up" is easier said than done, but it is when the times get tough that we as a group need to get tougher and smarter and more creative as a result. Do we all have our share of ups and downs? Sure, but, the thing to remember during the downs is to never give up. Having this trait will force you to think more creatively when things get difficult and don't always go as planned.

I'm reminded of a student of mine who told me that she had a weight on her chest because things seemed to be falling apart with a few deals. I was inspired, however, to hear her say that she was not about to give up. She said that she was going to do whatever it took to get the deals done. And if she lost the deals, she would accept that, but she wasn't about to give up for one second. Inspiring, isn't it? I had absolute faith that she would get things worked out with those few deals, and be stronger and smarter and more creative as a result. She got them done and ended up netting a profit of $56,000 in one day.

You see, my friend, success isn't delivered to you on a silver platter. It's taken me many years to become an overnight success. You have to work for your dreams and goals with everything you've got. You have to risk, adapt, change, grow, learn, and fight for everything you want. No one is going to do it for you, no matter how smart, pretty, handsome, or strong you think you are. And most important, *never give up*!

Throughout this book, my goal has been to educate and challenge you as you begin, systemize, and grow your real estate investing business. As you can probably see, I carry a very positive mindset, but also am not one to coddle those who I train in the details of this business. Real estate investing requires a backbone. It can be quite competitive, and even though competition is a good thing for any business, you need to be ready to face the competition with a full set of business weapons and ammunition.

Commit yourself to embracing, understanding, and implementing the skills and topics discussed within this book, and you will hands-down generate rapid success and longevity as well as separate yourself from those other real estate investors who might best be classified as wannabes. Remember, your microphone is always on when you are working your business. Clients of all shapes and sizes will be listening, and they will be evaluating you – be ready. Second, never forget why you are in this business. Sure, it is a great way to make some huge money, passive income, and long-term wealth, but you should love what you do as well. Try not to forget that part, because many investors often do and as a result lose steam over the long haul.

As promised, I would like for you to now complete the same questionnaire I had you do in the beginning of this book. I ask you to answer the questions honestly, so now we can see what progress you have made. When you're done, compare your results with the first round and make note of which areas you improved in and to what extent. Again, this assignment is meant to help you better understand yourself and your real estate investing business.

QUESTIONNAIRE (ROUND 2)

On a scale of 1 to 10, with 1 being the worst and 10 being the best, circle your answer:

I would rank my current understanding and development of a professional support team a:

1 2 3 4 5 6 7 8 9 10

I would rank my current level of real estate investment education a:

1 2 3 4 5 6 7 8 9 10

I would rank my positive attitude as a real estate investor a:

1 2 3 4 5 6 7 8 9 10

I would rank my current understanding of the necessary skills as a real estate investor a:

1 2 3 4 5 6 7 8 9 10

I would rank my current passion for real estate investing a:

1 2 3 4 5 6 7 8 9 10

I would rank my current professional appearance as a real estate investor a:

1 2 3 4 5 6 7 8 9 10

I would rank my current office set-up for my real estate business a:

1 2 3 4 5 6 7 8 9 10

I would rank my current accumulation of credentials and testimonials for my business a:

1 2 3 4 5 6 7 8 9 10

I would rank my current real estate transactional experience a:

1 2 3 4 5 6 7 8 9 10

I would rank my current understanding and development of a professional business plan a:

1 2 3 4 5 6 7 8 9 10

I would rank my current marketing plan for my real estate business a:

1 2 3 4 5 6 7 8 9 10

I would rank my current understanding of and approach to effective meetings a:

1 2 3 4 5 6 7 8 9 10

I would rank my current understanding and mastery of
real estate paperwork a:

1 2 3 4 5 6 7 8 9 10

I would rank my current understanding of and commitment to
customer service a:

1 2 3 4 5 6 7 8 9 10

I would rank my current tax/corporate structure for my
real estate business a:

1 2 3 4 5 6 7 8 9 10

I would rank my current understanding and pursuit of private lending a:

1 2 3 4 5 6 7 8 9 10

I would rank my overall credibility as a real estate investor a:

1 2 3 4 5 6 7 8 9 10

DO YOU CONSIDER YOURSELF SAVVY?

Over the Labor Day weekend of 2009, I got together with some relatives on my side of the family that I hadn't seen in years. During the visit I got to talking with my paternal grandfather. We got to talking about politics and real estate and the economy and small businesses and entrepreneurship, etc., and it was a very enjoyable conversation. It is almost refreshing in a way to listen to someone speak their mind when they have such knowledge about life and history and everyday facts.

During this conversation, my grandfather mentioned a word and then described it to me. The word was "savvy," and he then described it as, "to have a clear understanding of something, and a knowledge, and a confident level of common sense." He was clearly very intent on getting his point across to me about the importance of being savvy in life and business. After concluding the conversation with him, I continued to think about the true power and relevance of the word savvy.

If you look up the word savvy in the dictionary, it pretty much gives you the exact definition that my grandfather gives, to have a practical know-how, understanding and a mental grasp, as well as common sense of what it is that you do. So as I relate this to real estate investing, I want to ask you, do you consider yourself a savvy real estate investor/entrepreneur? If someone asked me that, I would confidently be able to say "yes." I wouldn't have always been able to say this, but as my experiences in real estate and business grew and continues to grow, my savvy has grown, too.

So what's the point of all this savvy talk? The point is that savvy is a vital and essential ingredient in your recipe to achieve success as an ultimate real estate investor. Without savvy you will always be just mediocre at best. The good news is that savvy can be acquired and nurtured. The more you know, the more experiences you have, the more you get out and do things that others aren't willing to do, the more savvy you will become as a real estate investor. Anyone in the world, past or present, who has made a name for themselves in business exemplified a high level of savvy. They have a strong understanding of their business and a mental grasp about what needs to be done to achieve success.

FACE YOUR FEAR – FORTUNE IS NEAR

Everybody in life encounters the emotion of fear. Fear is not a bad thing. It exists for our protection as an early warning signal. But what you need to understand is there is a very big difference between the healthy fear that tells people to avoid falling off a cliff and the fear that causes constraint, anxiety, stress, and keeps you from reaching your fullest potential.

Overcoming fear is a key element in achieving ultimate real estate investing success, in making your dreams come true, in making fortunes.

The first step to conquering your fear is to take a step back and attempt to understand exactly what it is that's keeping you from reaching your goals. What exactly is keeping you awake at night? What exactly are you afraid of? What are these fears that are inside you that are keeping you from obtaining your financial dreams?

One of the many detrimental things about fear is that it can and will do everything in its power to stop you before you get started. Fear has a complete imagination of its own, which is influenced only by negative emotions. If you let your fears take hold of you and constrain you, then all your ability to create and achieve will be crippled and potentially lost forever.

So, conquering fear is about controlling your state of mind. Instead of waking up each day and fearing the worst, you need to start reaching and aspiring for the absolute best. I believe the opposite of fear is faith, confidence, and courage. A mind that is filled with faith and confidence and courage can much more clearly see through the negative fog that prevents people from achieving their dreams. I mention faith here because I personally and strongly believe faith to be the antidote to fear. Fight fear with faith and never give up on your dreams.

More than anything else, your fears are made by you and what you choose to believe and how you choose to live your life. If you have to rid yourself of certain bad habits in order to eliminate and rise above your fears, then by all means do it. If you have to remove yourself from certain people in your life in order to rise above and defeat your fears, then do it. Nobody said this was going to be easy, but once you face your fear, fortune is near.

BRIAN'S JOURNAL ENTRY

"Do Your Best and Let God Do the Rest"

My wife, Danielle, and I were watching TV one night and we came across a show called LA Ink. If you're not familiar with this show, it is a reality show based in a tattoo parlor in Los Angeles, Calif., and is filled with your regular reality-TV drama, but I must say it was kind of interesting to watch. And some of the tattoos that these artists were drawing were pretty amazing.

I don't have any tattoos, and I've never really had any desire to get one; however, while we were watching this show, I told my wife that if I ever did get a tattoo, it would have to be one that really meant something to me and connected with me on a deep level. Then after thinking a little longer about what I might consider getting if I ever got one, I decided on a saying that I repeat to myself many times during a given day or week. That saying is, "Do your best and let God do the rest."

It's important for you to know, and I'm extremely proud to say, that I am an immersed believer and devout Christian. And this little saying is one that I like to personally live my life by, because I always want to stay focused and grounded in my faith.

This little saying is extremely powerful and reassuring. When I say it to myself, it gives me confidence and strength during times when I feel stressed and weak. You see, we all go through challenging times on a regular basis. It doesn't matter if you are black, white, red, yellow, whoever you might be. It doesn't matter if you have $100 in your bank or $1,000,000. We all put our pants on one leg at a time, we all need to wear deodorant in order to keep BO in check, we all enjoy a good dinner and a movie, we all go to bed at night and wake up to the same sun the next day. We are all 99.99% genetically the same.

What keeps me going in business and life during times when 99.99% of others would give up is my faith. You see, I believe that as long as I do my best and everything in my power to do my best, be positive and a good person, work hard to grow my business financially, I believe unquestionably that if I do my best, God will do the rest.

So as I come full circle, I don't plan to get a tattoo any time soon. But if I did get one, you now know what it would say. Instead, I'll stick to keeping my little saying on a Post-it note next to my desk where I can see it every day.

If you feel that my message "Do your best and let God do the rest" could be beneficial in helping you to get through the challenges of your business and life, then please feel free to take it and make it your own.

MAKE INVESTMENTS THAT HELP YOU GROW

When was the last time that you invested in yourself? I mean seriously invested in yourself in a way that would help you grow your business and learn new things and make more money as a result? If your answer to these questions is never, then I'm sorry to say this, but I feel bad for you. I know, I know but you have good reasons for not investing in yourself and your business education such as: you don't have the money, or you don't have enough time, or perhaps you think you already know it all and that any new investment in yourself would be a waste of money. The fact is, my friends, those are all poor excuses.

So let's dissect this investing in yourself concept. What exactly does it mean? It means taking educated risks and perhaps spending money or time or energy on something with the end result being it makes you better! Here are some examples of investing in yourself, all of which I have done and/or continue to do on a regular basis:

1. Investing in your real estate education by going to training boot camps held by qualified individuals.

2. Investing in real estate training materials *and implementing them*!

3. Investing in a real estate coach or mentor to help you through difficult deals and situations. *(This can be life-changing.)*

4. Investing in an assistant to help you with the everyday details and minutia that you encounter as a real estate investor.

5. Investing in the expansion of your business and moving to an office location.

6. Investing in your marketing (this is a big one that most people consider an expense vs. an investment).

7. Investing in new books, newsletters, self-help, and motivational materials.

8. Investing in something that helps you relieve stress. such as a vacation or a motorcycle (my personal favorite). There is nothing like cruising backcountry roads on a day with blue skies.

I'll never forget the first really big investment that I made in myself. I spent a little more than $30,000 in a real estate investing program, and looking back, although it seemed crazy to spend that kind of money on education, it also seemed so right to me inside. Does that make sense? Well, the truth of the matter is this: I couldn't afford not to make the investment in myself because it is knowledge and education that I can act on for the rest of my life. The good news is that I made my money back multiple times over, and looking back, I know that had I not made that decision to invest in my real estate investing education that I would not be where I am today, writing this book and sharing my experiences with you.

I'd like to leave you with two great quotes in regards to investing in yourself:

1. *"I don't ask how much it costs, I ask how much it will make me."* – Donald Trump

2. *"The price of education is cheap compared to the cost of ignorance."* – Ron LeGrand

As a final point, remember that despite real estate investing being a somewhat unique and creative profession, you do have support and guidance out there, so be sure to utilize the free resources that I've provided to you in this book and keep things moving in a forward direction at all times.

Your choices now are simple. Option 1, do nothing today, and continue along the same path of one step forward and two steps back. This is obviously the easiest choice because it's the path of least resistance, but it's by far the most costly. Option 2, quit letting thousands of dollars slip away and make a commitment to yourself that you will learn how to get rich with real estate.

BRIAN'S ULTIMATE RESOURCE

You may now consider me a part of your support network. Please reread this book as often as needed to reinforce the knowledge you must have to be as successful as I know you can and will be. Remember you are not alone, and to prove it to you, I want you to take the next step and go to www.FreeMakeMoneyGift.com to get all the free resource materials that I mentioned throughout this book and much more. Supplies are limited and you only pay shipping and handling, I'll take care of the rest.

Or, if you have any specific questions or comments about this book, real estate investing, entrepreneurship, or life in general all you need to do is send a fax to 859-201-1441. I want to know your thoughts, fears, goals, dreams, aspirations, and challenges. The ball is now in your court.

It has been a pleasure bringing this important money-making information to you and I wish you the very best in success. You are well on your way to becoming an ultimate real estate investor!

To Your Ultimate Success,

Brian T. Evans Jr.

Summary of
BRIAN'S KEY POINTS

- Once you create a system for getting your phone to ring, everything else will fall into place.

- If you want people to believe in the message that you are saying, they must first believe in you.

- Make sure that you don't ever become dependent on any one team member. When you become dependent on someone, then you can become trapped within your business. Always have other alternatives to consider.

- I recommend only using banker-borrowed money for short-term transactions. Avoid getting a new mortgage each time you want to buy a house. Personally guaranteed debt can be very dangerous!

- Be careful not to become obsessed with cost control and deductions. As the business owner, your job is to always focus on revenue, while your CPA can focus on reducing your cut to Uncle Sam.

- When you pay people promptly they will be much more inclined to respond to future requests promptly and refer new business to you.

- An appraisal is only someone's opinion. The true value of a property is what a buyer is willing to pay.

- Do only what you do best and let someone else do the rest.

- There may be no better educational investment than the investment in a qualified mentor/coach to help you grow your business.

- You must constantly invest in your education as a real estate investor if you want to achieve great success and longevity.

- A commitment to a favorable outcome is also referred to as a win-win situation.

- If you do nothing else when prescreening sellers, make sure that you determine the (1) ARV – after repaired value (2) asking price (3) loan information (4) repairs needed (5) reason for selling.

- If you do nothing else when prescreening buyers, make sure that you determine (1) What is the most they can pay for the down payment? (2) What is the most they can afford to pay monthly? (3) Is their credit good, bad, or ugly?

- If you take away anything from the section on negotiation let it be this, you will never get what you don't ask for.

- There are lots of ways to buy and lots of ways to sell. Always remember that the better you get at buying, the easier it is to sell and make money.

- Fall in love with the numbers, not the house.

- My best suggestion is to approach each and every deal you do as if you have zero mone or credit and therefore have to structure the deal accordingly to make it work. This forces you to think creatively and, as a result to minimize personal risk. Therefore, always remember that everytime you write a check you are at risk.

- Focus on making lots of money before you start making lots of changes.

- Time and circumstances often changes people's minds, so always leave the door open with clients.

- Always have your attorney review your paperwork to make sure that (1) It is your-state-"friendly" and (2) Your attorney is comfortable with everything.

- Only do business with people who want to do business with you. Manage your relationships with this attitude and things will be much simpler.

- Remember, your duty as a business owner and real estate investor is to focus on revenue, not cost control.

- When working with private lenders, always strive to under-promise and over-deliver.

- When things go wrong (and they will) correct the problem as quickly as possible, learn from it, and move on.

- Always remember, you are an investor and the only way you buy houses is if you can enter the deal with little or no money down and find a way to make a substantial profit with minimal risk. Otherwise you have no reason to get involved in the deal.

TreeNeutral

Advantage Media Group is proud to be a part of the Tree Neutral™ program. Tree Neutral offsets the number of trees consumed in the production and printing of this book by taking proactive steps such as planting trees in direct proportion to the number of trees used to print books. To learn more about Tree Neutral, please visit **www.treeneutral. com.** To learn more about Advantage Media Group's commitment to being a responsible steward of the environment, please visit **www. advantagefamily.com/green**

How To Make Money In Your Local Real Estate Market is available in bulk quantities at special discounts for corporate, institutional, and educational purposes. To learn more about the special programs Advantage Media Group offers, please visit **www. KaizenUniversity.com** or call 1.866.775.1696.

Advantage Media Group is a leading publisher of business, motivation, and self-help authors. Do you have a manuscript or book idea that you would like to have considered for publication? Please visit **www.amgbook.com**

The Most Incredible Real Estate Money Making Gift on the Planet Guaranteed ($1,966.94 Value)!

FREE

Jam-Packed with everything you see here. Limited Time Offer. Act Now!

($1,966.94 Value)

Incredible Free Gift Part 1 of 3

12 Free Months of Brian's "Ultimate Make Money Hotsheet" mailed to your doorstep, no strings attached. ($297 value)!

Incredible Free Gift Part 2 of 3

Free CD Download: 1 Hr. Interview with Brian about his 5 Guaranteed Steps to Small Business Success ($49 value)!
"This is the most powerful interview I've ever done." - Brian Evans

Incredible Free Gift Part 3 of 3

Free 30 minute 1-on-1 Make Money in Real Estate Jump Start Conference Call withBrian Evans. (value = Priceless)!
Students have said that this call was the most important and influential call of their entire real estate investing career. Brian typically charges $500/hr for consultations, however for a limited time you can speak to him FREE.

Course Manual and CD Set, "The 77 Biggest Mistakes Real Estate Investors Make ($997 value)!
The quality of information contained in this course is so content rich that everyone from those just starting, all the way up to the established real estate investor will benefit from the proven methods and mistakes to avoid.

Brian's Library of his 50 Most Commonly Used Real Estate Investing Forms ($387 value)!
This is a CD-Rom which you can put in your computer and print forms out at your leisure. Be sure to have your attorney review and approve the forms and make them "your state friendly."

Lifetime Access to "Foreclosure Gold Rush Live" Website ($39.97 value)!
If you've ever entertained the thought of investing in real estate and making a tremendous fortune in foreclosures, then this online program will show you the secrets.

Everything You Need To Attract Private Lenders ($147 value)!
I give you the most common and essential documents that I use to attract and work with private mortgage lenders in my real estate investing business. When utilized properly, private lenders will make you a lot of money and in return you'll provide them a very good return on investment.

E

Six Month Access to "What Would Evans Do" (WWED) Fax Back Hotline (value = Priceless)!
Have questions that need answers? No problem. Send your questions to my fax back hotline and I'l respond to you usually within 24 hours. This gift allows you to get inside my head, and therefore I can't even begin to put a price tag on this.

more

One Full Month Membership to Ultimate Real Estate Investors VIP Membership ($49.97 value)!

THIS IS THE ULTIMATE PLACE where Real Estate Investors from all over North America come together to Make Money, Live Wealthy, No Excuses."

TOP SECRET MONTHLY "VIP NEWSLETTERS" 20+ page Newsletters, referred to as a day long intense seminar in print arriving by first class mail.

EXCLUSIVE CD's OF THE MONTH. These are exclusive monthly CD's about keeping up with what's new, and other how to make money in real estate (without money, credit, or experience) tips.

SPECIAL VIP OPEN LINE WEEKLY CONFERENCE CALLS. Get first hand advice with weekly call in times to discuss deals, asset protection, contracts, sellers, buyers, etc!

NEW ➤ *PARTNERSHIP PROFITS. If you want, I will personally partner with you on your real estate deals: helping you get commitments, structure contracts, and close your deals. My personal money may or may not be used, case by case.*

DEAL STRUCTURING ADVICE. Each month you can fill out my UPS (Ultimate Prescreening Sellers) Sheet or my UPB (Ultimate Prescreening Buyers) Sheet and fax them to my office for direct input on how you should approach and structure each deal that you are considering. It's like having a real estate angel on your shoulder!

VIP MEMBERS' RESTRICTED ACCESS WEBSITE: A section of the website contains past issues of the TOP SECRET VIP Newsletter, articles, special news, etc. ONLY VIP Members are given the access code for this website.

CONTINUALLY UP-DATED "MILLION DOLLAR RESOURCE DIRECTORY: There are contacts and resources that myself and clients use - and in many cases, have found only after diligent and difficult search.

20% DISCOUNT ON FUTURE PRODUCTS AND EVENTS

OTHER SPECIAL PERKS and call in hours ONLY for VIP Members

************* I TOLD YOU IT WAS INCREDIBLE! *************

There is a one-time charge of $19.95 to cover shipping and handling for everything with free gift 3 of 3. After your 1 month free test drive as a VIP Member you will automatically continue at the lowest VIP Member price of $49.97 per month. Should you decide to cancel your membership, you can do so at any time by calling our office at 859-309-1714. Remember, your credit card will NOT be charged the low monthly membership fee until the begining of the 2nd month, which means you will receive 1 full month of all benefits outlined above to read, test, and profit from all of the powerful techniques and strategies you get from being an Ultimate Real Estate Investor "VIP" Member. **You Can't Lose Guarantee** - And of course, it's impossible for you to lose, because if you don't absolutely LOVE everything you get, simply call 859-309-1714 and we'll even refund your S&H.

*EMAIL REQUIRED IN ORDER TO NOTIFY YOU ABOUT YOUR ORDER

Full Name

Billing Address

City   State   Zip   *Email

Phone   Fax

Credit Card Instructions to Cover $19.95 Shipping & Handling:

_____Visa _____MasterCard _____American Express _____Discover

Credit Card Number:_____ Exp. Date_____

Signature_____ Date_____

Order Online at www.FreeMakeMoneyGift.com
Or Fax Back to 859-201-1441
Or Mail To: 3070 Lakecrest Circle 400-260 Lexington, KY 40513

Printed in the USA
CPSIA information can be obtained
at www.ICGtesting.com
JSHW012021140824
68134JS00033B/2813